ENGLISH ❖ HERITAGE

Book of
Lindisfarne

Holy Island

ENGLISH ✠ HERITAGE

Book of
Lindisfarne
Holy Island

Deirdre O'Sullivan and
Robert Young

B.T. Batsford Ltd/English Heritage
London

First published 1995

Typeset by Lasertext Ltd, Stretford,
Manchester M32 0JT
and printed in Great Britain by
The Bath Press, Bath

Published by B T Batsford Ltd
4 Fitzhardinge Street, London W1H 0AH

A CIP catalogue record for this book is
available from the British Library

ISBN 0 7134 7307 X (cased)
0 7134 7229 4 (limp)

Contents

Illustrations

Colour plates

Preface

This book aims to provide a basic guide to what is currently known about the archaeology and history of Lindisfarne. It is based partly on the fruits of our own endeavours in the field but also relies heavily on the work of many scholars and researchers who have engaged in both general and particular studies of the archaeology and history of northern England.

The idea of undertaking an intensive archaeological survey on the island was born in 1977, from a realization of how little practical fieldwork had actually been carried out there. Since then we have spent the equivalent of a year in the field, mostly in short Easter and slightly longer summer seasons, with teams of up to forty people. The number of students from Leicester and Lampeter Universities who have directly assisted in excavation, post-excavation and survey on Lindisfarne must now be numbered in their hundreds, and it is impossible to list them all here: we are particularly indebted to Peter Boyer, Nick Cooper, Sarah Crane, Nick Herepath, Shaun Hides, Susan Kruse, Irena Lentowicz, Heather Lomas, David Mackie, Sandra Ottaway, Toby Simpson, Nick Tulip and Kerry York for supervising various aspects of the work.

We are particularly grateful to Paul Beavitt, co-leader of the project for many years, and also Eric Cambridge and Kevin Walsh who have offered us contributions based on their own original research on various aspects of the island's history. The remainder of the book has been based on collaborative work; Deirdre O'Sullivan is responsible for Chapters 1, 4–5, and the overall editing of the text; Robert Young wrote Chapters 3 and 8 and co-ordinated the illustrations. The first part of Chapter 9 is a joint effort.

Permission to work on Lindisfarne has always been willingly given by the various individuals and bodies involved, and we would like to thank Major Humphrey Crossman, Jimmie Patterson and Robert Brigham, and English Nature and English Heritage, for their consent. We owe a special debt of gratitude to David O'Connor, for many years warden of the Northumberland Coast National Nature Reserve, and his successor, Phil Davey, who have shown great interest and given practical support, and David Sherlock and Bob Bewley, sometime English Heritage inspectors for the North-East.

A special debt is owed to the Revd Kate Tristram and the staff of Marygate House, and the many island residents who have taken an interest in our work and endured the vicissitudes of our visits, especially the Revd Dennis Bill, Jimmy Brigham, Len and Christine Cail, Ernie Evans, Ian and Ann McGregor, Sue and Clive Massey, Malcolm Patterson, Pauline and Dick Patterson and Fred Rose.

Many of our academic colleagues and friends have offered useful advice and positive encouragement over the years and we wish particularly to acknowledge the help of Marion Archibold, Richard Bailey, Ian Bailiff, Martin

Bell, Tony Brown, Rosemary Cramp, Peter Fowler, Tony Gouldwell, Graham Morgan, Elizabeth Pirie, James Rackham, Sue Stally-brass and Charles Thomas. We must also record our gratitude to the staff of the North-umberland Record Office, and the other individuals and bodies that provided us with illustrations and photographs.

Financial assistance for different aspects of the project has been received from a wide range of sources, including the University of Leicester and St David's University College, Lampeter, the Pan-tyfedwyn Fund of the University of Wales, English Heritage, English Nature and the Society for Medieval Archaeology.

The book was written at the suggestion of Graeme Barker, and we would like to thank him and all our other colleagues at Leicester who have helped it on its way, especially Sarah Beauchamp, Gurjit Dhillon, Tony Gouldwell, Deborah Miles, Sue Pike and Doug Smith. We are also grateful to Peter Dunn, Stephen Johnson, Sarah Vernon-Hunt and Peter Kemmis Betty of English Heritage and Batsford for much assistance and advice. Sue Vaughan produced the index at very short notice.

Deirdre O'Sullivan and
Robert Young
August 1994

1
Introduction

Lindisfarne, or Holy Island, Northumberland, is known throughout western Europe as the site of a famous early Christian monastery, founded in 635 by St Aidan, a monk of Iona. From here the Christian message was transmitted to the pagan Anglo-Saxons of northern Britain. Its name is synonymous with the 'Golden Age' of Northumbria, as recounted in the works of England's earliest and most celebrated historian, the Venerable Bede. In a sense it was also the place where this 'Golden Age' came to an end, as it was the scene of the first clearly documented Viking raid on the British Isles, in 793. Many famous treasures were produced in the Anglo-Saxon monastery, including what is usually considered to be the finest surviving illuminated English manuscript of the early Middle Ages, the Lindisfarne Gospels. Lindisfarne is also known as the home of St Cuthbert, the most famous of the Lindisfarne bishops, and the premier saint of northern England in the Middle Ages, whose relics are now on display in Durham Cathedral.

The Anglo-Saxon monastery was abandoned in the later ninth century as a result of Viking harassment, and in the later medieval period the island slipped into the backwaters of history, supporting a small village community. In veneration of St Cuthbert, a small Benedictine priory was refounded as a cell of Durham towards the end of the eleventh century.

Nowadays Lindisfarne has a fairly small permanent population, virtually all of whom live in the village on the south coast. Many of the inhabitants are now dependent on tourism for their livelihood, but the small fishing fleet reflects a more traditional way of earning a living. In the previous century a number of industrial enterprises were carried out on Lindisfarne, including lime extraction on a fairly substantial scale, and also coal mining, but for much of its recent history Lindisfarne supported a typical fishing and farming coastal community, although its strategic location attracted fortification in the sixteenth and seventeenth centuries, when the island played its own small part in the defence of the realm.

The name Lindisfarne is first found in the writings of Bede of the early eighth century; before the foundation of the Anglo-Saxon kingdom of Northumbria it may have been known as *Inis Metcaut*, a native British name which is used in later sources. The significance of the names is not absolutely clear. The Anglo-Saxon name may mean simply the island of the *Lindisfaran*, or people from Lindsey. Lindsey was the name of an Anglo-Saxon kingdom of the seventh century in the modern county of Lincolnshire; but there is no other reason to link the island with this area. An alternative, and probably wholly fanciful, interpretation was first proposed by Symeon of Durham in the twelfth century. He suggested that the first part of the name, *Lindis*, was a stream name, to which the element *farne*, meaning island, has been added. The island may thus have been

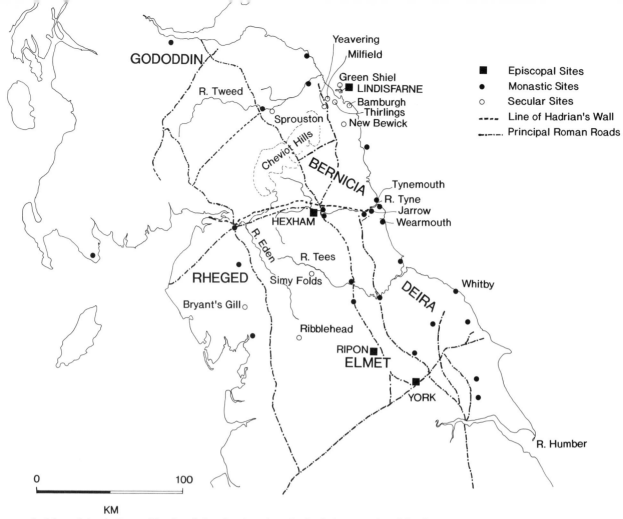

1 *Map of Anglo-Saxon Northumbria, showing the principal sites mentioned in the text.*

identified as one of the Farne Islands, a group of rocky islands off the coast of Northumberland, which are now usually reached from Seahouses. The modern name of Holy Island derives from the medieval *Insula Sacra*, a name invented by the monks of Durham in honour of its particular place in the early history of their community.

The island (**colour plate 2**) lies nearly 2km (1¼ miles) off the coast of Northumberland,

> …where the waves are eager to curl over the shore with grey water, but rush to lay them bare as they go to their backward course, and the blue depths encircle a sacred land, and afford a ready journey when they lay the shores bare…

as the ninth-century poet Aethelwulf elegantly describes it. Unlike the other islands in the

Farne group it is a tidal island, and can be reached on foot for a period of up to seven hours, twice a day at low tide. It is this intermittent accessibility which has given life on the island much of its unique character. It is tempting to see Lindisfarne as remote, but although it is distant from modern centres of population it has never been difficult to access. Unlike many other islands, its economy both now and in earlier times is interdependent with that of the adjacent mainland. Although most of the island is low-lying, the rock on which the castle was built is a striking landmark from many places along the coast, and fine views of the Northumbrian coastline and the Cheviot Hills, and the open sea to both the north and east, are in turn available on the island, from both the Castle Rock and the Heugh (see **25** and **68**), the basalt ridge which runs along part of the south coast. When the monastery was founded in the seventh century it was in fact placed on excellent lines of coastal communication with other important Northumbrian centres (**1**) and the royal site at Bamburgh would have loomed conspicuously on the horizon.

In shape the island resembles a small axe. The northern part (the axe handle) is known as the Snook; it is about 5km (3 miles) across and is now covered in sand dunes. The area of modern farmland is about 2sq.km ($\frac{3}{4}$ sq.mile) in extent, and corresponds to the blade of the axe. On the southern side of the island facing the mainland there is a wide natural shallow harbour known as the Ouse. Access to this from the sea can be difficult as there are a number of sandbars in the bay.

The modern causeway linking the mainland to the island at the shortest crossing-place consists of a metalled road and a small bridge. Before it was built the usual route across the sands ran from Beal to the place known as Chare Ends, where the main road on the island met the shore. This route is known as the Pilgrim's Way and it is clearly marked by a line of tall posts and refuge boxes, which have been regularly renewed, most recently in 1987 to commemorate the 1300th anniversary of St Cuthbert's death (**2**). The vestiges of earlier lines of posts mark out two other safe paths across the sands, one close to the line of the present causeway.

The completion of the causeway in 1954 resulted in a substantial increase of tourists, attracted by the scenery and wildlife and perhaps most of all by the lure of history. There are a number of ancient monuments on Lindisfarne, but very little survives above ground of the monastery of St Aidan and St Cuthbert, and visitors must spend a small amount of time on the island, in spite of the restrictions of the tides, if they are to gain some understanding of what it would have looked like in its heyday. The best-known survivals of the 'Golden Age' of Lindisfarne, the Gospels, the relics of St

2 *The Pilgrim's Way, with a reconstructed refuge box.*

Cuthbert and the collection of carvings in the priory museum, have been extensively, even exhaustively, studied as art objects, but they also need to be seen in their physical and cultural context. It is hoped that this book will help to provide that context, whether for those interested in Anglo-Saxon England, or for the modern visitor to the island itself. It also aims to draw attention to some other, lesser-known aspects of the island's history which are worthy of much more attention than they have hitherto received. Lindisfarne today is part of the Northumberland Coast National Nature Reserve, and planning restrictions have done much to preserve the character of the village and the richness of the island's plant and animal life.

Archaeology on Lindisfarne

Lindisfarne was a frequent stopping point for parties of antiquarian tourists in the later part of the nineteenth century, who took advantage of the services of the London and North Eastern Railway as far as Beal. Then, as now, enthusiasts were mostly drawn by the castle and the priory ruins, but there was also speculation about the Anglo-Saxon monastery, which was assumed to have been in the vicinity of the medieval priory. Some of them made interesting comments and observations although these did not necessarily make their way into print; a sketch plan made by one S.P. Blackwell, who

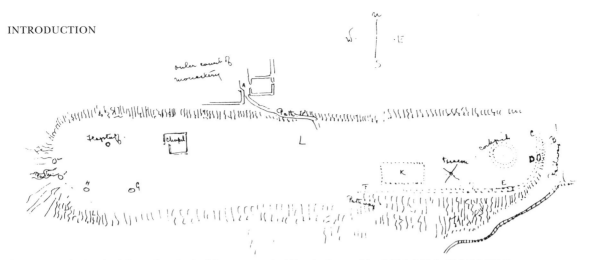

3 *Blackwell's sketch of the archaeological features on the Heugh observed in 1891 (NRO 683/10/133).*

visited the island in 1891 is shown in **3**. In a subsequent correspondence with Sir William Crossman, the principal landowner on the island, he drew attention to a group of shallow earthworks on the Heugh, previously very briefly noted by the historian James Raine. It is now appreciated that at least some of these earthworks may represent buildings of the Anglo-Saxon monastery, but although Crossman carefully kept his note, the vital information on the little sketch was never followed up or published.

The priory was the earliest focus of serious antiquarian interest. A number of early engravings show it in an appropriately ruined and romantic state (see **52** and **53**). As Crown property it was in the care of the Ministry of Fisheries and Woods in the nineteenth century when parts of the priory church were restored. It was not, however, until the last decade of that century that a programme of serious archaeological exploration was undertaken. This work was carried out by Sir William Crossman himself, who obtained permission from the Ministry of Works to excavate in the cloisters of the priory in order to recover the plan of the buildings and to see if any evidence for the early monastery survived. The actual survey was undertaken by the architect C.C. Hodges, known in the north of England for his work at Hexham Abbey. Sir William also explored the ruins on St Cuthbert's Island, the islet

off the south coast of Lindisfarne, which were not in Crown ownership. The excavations were done at Crossman's own expense, and conformed to the standards of the time: a short report was published by the Berwickshire Naturalist's Club. His permit only allowed the removal of deposits to the level of the floor of the nave, within the area of the cloister.

Crossman's published account of his excavations discussed the plan of the medieval cloister, and he was careful to relate his discoveries both to the buildings mentioned in the medieval priory accounts – many published by James Raine a few decades before – and also to the post-Dissolution use of the monastery. Although some of his identifications would now be challenged, many of them have stood the test of more recent scholarship. His report states that 'no relics of any great importance' were found during the excavations, but he does note that coins were found in the course of the work and an unusual life-sized lead model of a herring, which was found in the well in the outer court. Crossman was unsuccessful in his attempts to find any evidence of the Anglo-Saxon monastery under the priory, possibly because his excavations never penetrated through the later medieval layers.

On St Cuthbert's Island he recovered the plan of a single-celled rectangular chapel with an attached apartment, which he identified with the chapel of St Cuthbert-in-the-Sea, referred to in the priory documents at the Dissolution. He also noted a number of other archaeological features on the island. These consisted of a narrow, U-shaped ditch surrounding the eastern side of the chapel, which he interpreted as a breakwater, a low, circular mound to the north of the chapel, and, to the south-east of it and just above the high-water mark, a rectangular group of walls, which he saw as possibly the remains of a cell for the priest attached to the chapel. Just below this he identified the vestigial remains of 'much earlier work', possibly the site of the cell of St Cuthbert himself.

Subsequent to Crossman's work, the Ministry of Works itself undertook further clearance and restoration in the cloisters and nave of the priory in the early decades of the twentieth century (4). No further plans were published at the time, although some were drawn up, but the Inspector who had overall responsibility for the work, Charles Peers, wrote an account of the fragments of Anglo-Saxon carved stones which were found reused as building stones in the foundations of the later medieval priory. In the course of the restoration, a detailed stone-by-stone drawing of the nave was made, which enabled the close study of the surviving masonry fabric.

No systematic recording of the archaeological layers disturbed by this work was undertaken, but the quantities of broken medieval pottery recovered suggest that deposits of the twelfth to sixteenth centuries were removed. It is quite likely that the rather crude techniques of excavation might have failed to reveal the remains of Anglo-Saxon timber buildings, which can prove elusive even with modern methods. However, unlike the similar campaign of work at Whitby Abbey, also carried out under Peers' overall supervision, there were virtually no finds of the Anglo-Saxon period, apart from the reused carved stones. Some of these were grave markers, and this suggested at least that the early monastic cemetery must have been within the area of the medieval priory, but the precise site of the monastery buildings was still unclear.

In 1936, a prehistoric dimension to the island's past was added by Francis Buckley, who found an early Mesolithic microlithic point near the Castle Rock. A year later another casual visitor, W. de L. Aitcheson, excavated some disused hearth-sites in the dunes, at the north-west end of the Snook and near Snipe Point. He found nothing to date them, but it is probable that they relate to the post-medieval development of industry on Lindisfarne.

There has been no further archaeological exploration of the priory, but in the 1960s Dr Brian Hope-Taylor of the University of Cambridge carried out a programme of survey and small-scale excavation on the island, as part of a more general study of early Anglo-Saxon Northumbria, which included the excavation of the royal sites at Yeavering and Bamburgh. His work on Lindisfarne has remained unpublished, but it is understood that he uncovered some foundations on the western end of the Heugh and also some medieval buildings in a field to the west of the present vicarage.

4 *Ministry of Works excavation in progress in the priory cloisters in the early twentieth century (*English Heritage*)*

In 1977, a small excavation was carried out by Deirdre O'Sullivan on the present site of the English Heritage museum, immediately north of the parish church and priory ruins. This revealed a complex sequence of building use from the later Middle Ages through to the seventeenth century, together with part of an earlier building, which may have dated from the time of the Anglo-Saxon monastery.

Although archaeological work on Lindisfarne itself was fairly limited before the 1980s, the treasures of its 'Golden Age' have been extensively researched and the results published in scholarly works. The majority of these, perhaps fittingly, are associated with Durham, where the heirs to the Lindisfarne community still protect the relics of their patron saint. In 1940 a Reader in English at the University of Durham, Bertram Colgrave, produced a definitive edition of the two eighth-century *Vitae*, or Lives, of St Cuthbert, which brought detailed information about the early history of the island monastery to a wider audience. A facsimile edition of the Lindisfarne Gospels, accompanied by an exhaustive critical discussion of all aspects of the manuscript, was

published in 1956–60. The book thus became one of the most accessible and best-studied texts of the Middle Ages. The relics of St Cuthbert were also published in detail in 1956, although partly in response to changing methods of conservation and display, new work on these has continued to produce fresh discoveries. The collection of Anglo-Saxon sculpture from the island has also been the subject of exhaustive research by Rosemary Cramp, Professor of Archaeology at Durham, and in 1987, an international symposium on 'St Cuthbert, his cult and his community' was held in Durham to commemorate the 1300th anniversary of the saint's death.

This emphasis on St Cuthbert and his times is understandable, but restricting. The very wealth of material about Cuthbert may even have encouraged inertia on other matters. Scholars seemed to have tacitly accepted that there was nothing new to be found on Lindisfarne itself: the Anglo-Saxon monastery had been obliterated by the later Benedictine priory and there was little else of interest.

Fieldwork in the 1980s has shown, however, that nothing could be further from the truth. The majority of the contributors to this book have been involved in this work, the Lindisfarne

5 *Lindisfarne Research Project: location of sites.*

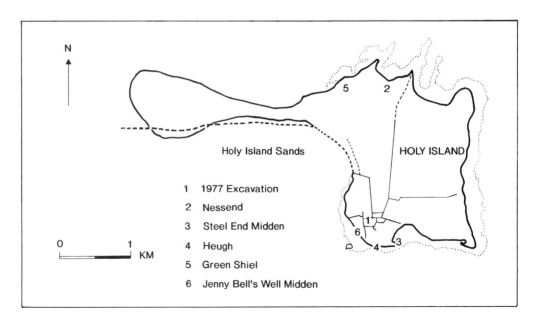

Holy Island Sands   HOLY ISLAND

1   1977 Excavation
2   Nessend
3   Steel End Midden
4   Heugh
5   Green Shiel
6   Jenny Bell's Well Midden

0   1
└─────────┘ KM

Research Project, which was inspired by a brief survey carried out in 1980; organized fieldwork began in 1983. Because of its very nature, the project has had to adopt a broadly based research strategy: the main aim is to investigate the settlement history of the island from the earliest times rather than a specific focus on the Anglo-Saxon monastery.

A number of new sites of different periods have been identified and the work has included field survey, excavation, documentary research and the study of aerial photographs. The work has involved both the identification and exploration of individual sites and a programme of environmental sampling, which has provided a more general picture of the island landscape, and changing land-use.

The sites explored so far (5) include a prehistoric scatter of flint and other worked stone at Nessend Quarry, an early medieval settlement at Green Shiel and a medieval midden and stone revetment on the foreshore opposite St Cuthbert's Island. An extensive programme of conventional and geophysical survey in and around the priory and a general survey of the industrial archaeology of the island have also been undertaken. The discovery of so much new material has been welcome, even though it provides an alarming index of the quantity of archaeological data still undiscovered in the landscape.

We have not of course been alone in our renewed interest in Lindisfarne: the number of visitors to the island increases annually, and this has led to the construction of the new museum, which replaced a much simpler display in the outbuildings of the Manor House Hotel. It was opened by St Cuthbert's then successor as Bishop of Durham, David Jenkins, in 1987. The display concentrates on finds from the Anglo-Saxon and medieval priory, but some of the material from recent archaeological fieldwork is also on show. It offers an excellent starting point for a study of the history and archaeology of the island. However, a walk around the harbour or along the Heugh will greatly enhance any visitor's appreciation of the monastic setting: the low, open landscape, the clear light and the superb vistas of the North Sea and Northumberland coast would have formed the backdrop to the 'Golden Age' as much as in the present day

2
The changing environment of Lindisfarne

Human activity in any place is obviously affected by the local environment and natural resources available. In early periods of history, such factors would have been far more important than they are today as communications would not have been anything like as extensive. That is not to say that Lindisfarne was ever without links with the mainland; there has probably always been some kind of communication, both economic and social, with other people and places in the immediate hinterland, and indeed further afield. However, for most of the island's history the majority of people would have been at least partly reliant on what the climate and the natural resources on the island could offer. Some might argue that people's lives were largely dictated by these factors, but it would probably be fairer to see the environment and resources of Lindisfarne as presenting the inhabitants with a range of opportunities.

It is sometimes assumed that the environment, especially the climate and the topography, have remained the same throughout history. This has never been so, especially on Lindisfarne where the changing influences of the sea and the sand have had varying effects throughout the centuries. The environment has not only altered as a result of climatic factors; human activity has also had a very important impact, and the impact of both of these on such a small place has been quite marked.

Throughout Lindisfarne's long history most natural resources have been exploited at one time or another; from the fish and mammals of the sea, to the waders and sea birds, to the soil and the plants and trees, to the very rocks of which the island is formed. This chapter will consider the history of these resources, and how the environment has changed over time – how the climate has affected it and how people have exploited it.

Geology and geomorphology
The first and most logical place to start when considering the environmental history of any place is the geology, the basic mineral strata from which the island is made, together with the subsequent development of its geomorphology – the nature of the physical topography and the processes which contribute to its formation. Again, it is important to realize that the geomorphology of a place is never static: environmental processes continually contribute towards a changing landscape. On Lindisfarne this is especially true of the northern part of the island, an area dominated by sand dunes which have altered the face of the island during the last five hundred years.

Regional geology (6)
In northern Northumberland the Cheviot Hills, formed from granite and andesite, are a dominant feature. These emerged during a volcanic episode about 400 million years ago. Characteristic of this area are the grass-covered hills

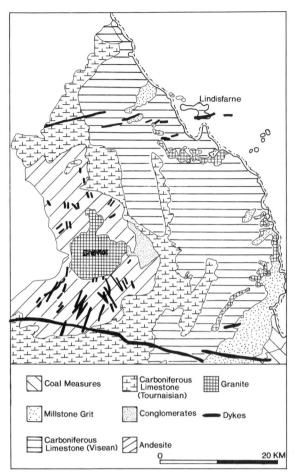

6 *Map of regional geology of north-eastern Northumberland (after British Geological Survey).*

and valleys which cut the granite rocks and the lava pile. Moving east from the Cheviots towards the coastal plain, carboniferous geology is encountered; these rocks were lain down some 300 million years ago, and include cementstone and fell sandstones. This part of north-east England is characterized by the streams and rivers which flow out over the plain. Moving further east towards the coast, the middle and lower limestones are met, many laid down during the early part of the carboniferous period. These deposits were broken only by the relatively numerous outcrops of whin sill and dykes, dolerite intrusions about 300 million years old. One of the best-known dykes is the Holy Island echelon which is visible on

the southern side of the island, as the Heugh and the Castle Rock.

On top of these rocks the next important geological event would have been the laying down of drift deposits: sediments, often clay, which were deposited by glaciers moving over the area between 2 million and 10,000 years ago. It is these deposits which form the basis for many of the modern soils and sediments which constitute an important part of the environment today. No part of this region was left unaffected by glaciation, and large areas of the north-east are covered with glacial drift deposits. Such deposits reach a maximum thickness of about 92m (300ft) in County Durham, though they are usually no more than about 15m (50ft) thick over the rest of the region. These deposits have had a profound effect on the topography of the lowlands in this part of England: much of the coastal area is only above sea level today as a result of the thickness of the drift deposits and is characterized by a relatively featureless or irregularly undulating topography.

In considering the tombolo of Lindisfarne (the correct term for a tidal island) the first characteristic to note is that it is geologically a continuation of the middle limestone formations of north-east Northumberland (**7**). Prior to the current environmental period, known as the Holocene, or post-glacial era, which began about 10,000 years ago, Lindisfarne would not have been an island at all. To the south of Lindisfarne, the southern North Sea area would have been a continuous land-bridge linking a large part of eastern England with northern Europe. This land-bridge had its northern limit between northern Norfolk and Texel in the south Waddenzee area of the Netherlands and this section of the coast of north-east England may have been a further 6km (4 miles) out from the modern coastline at this time (see **15**). With the melting of the glaciers and the consequent rising of sea levels, Lindisfarne would have begun to take on its modern shape, although it would still have been very different

19

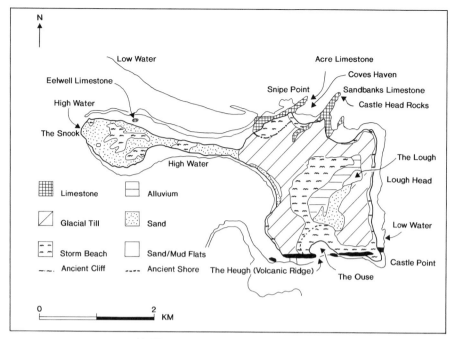

7 *The geomorphology of Lindisfarne.*

in many other ways. Even after the glaciers had disappeared and the tombolo had formed, sea levels would have carried on changing, as they are even today.

Such changes are the product of two opposing processes: the first is the slow lifting of an

8 *The raised beach near the priory, seen from the Heugh. This marks an earlier shoreline on Lindisfarne, and may have been one boundary of the early medieval monastery.*

entire landmass as a result of the reduction of downward pressure put on the land by the ice sheets of the glaciation (isostatic uplift). Despite the fact that the last glaciation ended about 10,000 years ago, large areas of land are still experiencing such uplift. On Lindisfarne this is testified to by the existence of a raised beach on the eastern shore of the island (**8**). The second process is also linked to the ending of the last glaciation: sea levels in many areas are rising

because of the increase of water in the oceans as ice sheets melt. In Northumberland, more than anywhere else in Britain, there is a race between the uplifting of the land and the rising sea levels. While there is no doubt that many parts of this region have experienced uplift, sea levels in relative terms have increased at a faster rate. A low-lying island, Lindisfarne is potentially threatened by rising sea levels. Global temperatures are predicted to rise between 0.5°C and 2.5°C by the year 2030, and this could increase the rate of melting of the polar ice caps. In these circumstances the race between the uplift of the land and rising sea levels in Northumberland will easily be won by the sea. There are of course many uncertainties about the models for sea level rise, but there is little doubt that Lindisfarne will be affected during the next century, although the exact extent cannot be predicted at present.

The sequence of rock strata on Lindisfarne

Despite its small size, Lindisfarne possesses a varied geology. The oldest rocks on the island only surface to the north of the Snook; here the Eelwell limestone can be seen at low tide as an area less than 200m (650ft) wide. The next layers of rocks in this sequence are shales, but these are not visible anywhere on the island. Then comes the Acre limestone, which can be seen easily along the north shore. In many ways, this is one of the most important rocks on the island – it has been used by the islanders for building material since at least the early medieval period and was extensively quarried for lime-burning during the nineteenth century. More shales follow the limestone in this chronological sequence and these can be seen on the northern part of the island at Coves Haven, and on the south immediately south of the Heugh.

The youngest rocks on Lindisfarne are a sequence of sandstones interrupted by yet another layer of limestone. The oldest of these sandstones are visible as near vertical cliffs at the eastern end of Coves Haven. The final layer of limestone is known as Sandbanks limestone which appears on the north shore of the island as the Castlehead Rocks. Immediately to the south of this outcrop is the now disused quarry at Nessend, a testament to the extensive working of these rocks during the nineteenth century. The Sandbanks limestone is also visible on the south of the island below the eastern section of the volcanic intrusion. The youngest rocks are more sandstones, which are found on the eastern shore of the island at Lough Head.

In many ways the most important geological features are the youngest superficial deposits such as the glacial till (clay) which covers much of the island (see 7). The other important superficial deposits are the storm beaches. At some point during its history Lindisfarne was probably split into three or more parts, attested to by the existence of storm beaches and alluvium at different points. Storm beaches are sediments of coarse sand and gravel that have been moved by extreme storms. The piling up of such material can obviously contribute to the formation of new areas of land, and, in the case of Lindisfarne, link together previously separate areas, or areas that were often breached by the sea during high tides and storms – the Snook was such an area. The main body of the island was also split by high sea levels which covered the area where the storm beach and alluvium were deposited. However, the island was eventually consolidated by the deposition of this storm beach material, probably over a period of time rather than during one extreme event. As well as coarse sediments, alluvium has also been deposited on the island north of the Ouse, the island's harbour.

At some point after these events, and possibly during the last 1000 years, the size of the Ouse was reduced by the continuation of these sedimentation processes. As sediments were washed in by the sea, the area of dry land on this part of the island increased in size. Today a marshy area above the visible storm beach is evident. Above this marshy area is a terrace, the edge of which is clearly defined by a curving bank just to the east of the priory and the limit of the village (see **8**). It is quite likely that this is the line of the old shore, and that the priory and the village were rather closer to the sea than they are today.

The Ouse has maintained its current characteristics for some centuries now, although the water level is probably a lot lower than it has been; it is not rare for the Lough to dry out completely during the summer. The island possesses a few springs and wells, one of the more famous being Jenny Bell's Well. However, these alone are not enough to sustain the population, and piped water was first brought to the islanders in 1955; the water tower near Lewins Lane testifying to this important development.

Another important environmental process which has profoundly altered the island in relatively recent history is the development of the sand dune system along the north coast. Sand dune systems are one of the most 'plastic' environment types on the planet: their shape and location can alter dramatically over very short periods of time. Only when sand dunes have been fixed by the planting of tough grasses, especially marram grass, can they be controlled, and even then pressure by humans and extreme climatic events can still result in sudden and dramatic change.

There is much evidence to support the belief that there has not always been such an extensive dune system on Lindisfarne. There have undoubtedly been periods when sand has blown across the northern part of the island and small dunes may have appeared, but the dune system as it stands today probably did not develop until the fifteenth or sixteenth centuries. One of the most important pieces of evidence supporting the relatively recent development of the dune system is the existence of the Anglo-Saxon farmstead at Green Shiel, a site now within the dune system (Chapter 7). Work in and around this site has shown that it was located at the top of the beach on relatively

fine sand that would have been blown by winds that were not as strong as those which formed the modern sand dunes. The farmstead is less than 30m (100ft) from the edge of the glacial clay cliff. This cliff forms the edge of a wide, flat expanse of clay and a soil has formed directly on top of this, immediately behind the farmstead. This soil was put to agricultural usage during the medieval period, a fact which is most obviously supported by the existence of ridges and furrows which run in a south–south-east to north–north-west direction. The creation of ridges and furrows by farmers ploughing during the medieval period is a common occurrence throughout Britain and Europe. This system was probably used to help with drainage, as the soil in this area especially would have been quite wet. Today, this soil is buried beneath about 1m (3ft) of blown sand, which was probably deposited when the present sand dune system first developed.

During the ninth and tenth centuries AD much of Europe experienced a climatic optimum, a warmer period with fewer storms. On Lindisfarne support for this theory comes from a rather unlikely source: the whelk. Whelks are a useful indicator of the level of wave action on a shoreline and **9** shows both an elongated and a squat whelk. Longer whelks, with a relatively large total length to aperture-height ratio, tend to occupy beaches with a low level of wave action, while squatter whelks with a lower ratio, live on more exposed beaches with more vigorous waves. The whelks on the North Shore of Lindisfarne today tend to be of the

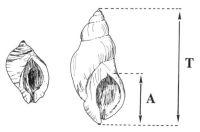

9 *Diagram showing the difference between squat and elongated whelks. The total length to aperture ratio is T/A.*

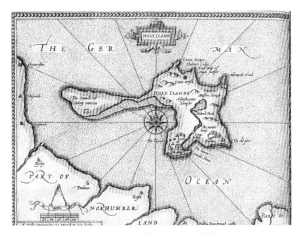

10 *The Speed map of Lindisfarne, 1610.*

squatter variety, but those recovered from early medieval deposits at the farmstead are undeniably longer. It is quite probable that the North Shore during the early medieval period was not as exposed as it is today and that there were not as many heavy storm events. The intensity of storm events, especially wind levels, is of great importance in the formation of dunes, as it is the powerful storms which shift the greatest amount of sand, and thus form sand dune systems. By the middle of the fifteenth century most of Europe was experiencing frequent and intense storms, and it is at this time that many dune systems either expanded or developed afresh; a number of coastal places in the North Sea region were overwhelmed by blown sand.

We can be sure that a relatively impressive dune system had developed on Lindisfarne by the end of the sixteenth century, as the first map of the island, published in 1610 by John Speed (**10**) clearly indicates the existence of such a system along the north coast. At the end of the nineteenth century the geological survey of Lindisfarne noted that the highest dunes were some 65ft (20m) above the sea. This is lower than the recorded height of the highest dunes today (*c.* 24m (78ft)) though it does not imply any great difference in the extent and size of the dune area and the dunes within it.

Even when the dunes had developed they

would have been very unstable, shifting location over relatively short periods of time and threatening nearby settlements and agricultural land. The planting of marram grass became a common practice during the later medieval period, after the storms of the fifteenth and sixteenth centuries had caused sand dunes to encroach on a number of coastal settlements all over Britain. In 1742, what can probably be considered the first conservation act in Britain was passed, specifically to protect this grass: it made uprooting it a criminal offence.

Despite the planting of marram grass on Lindisfarne, large parts of the dune system have been unstable until fairly recent times. Air photographs taken since 1954 indicate that the area around Green Shiel, for example, did not take on its current appearance until the 1960s. Prior to this it seems that the settlement site, as well as the remains of a fishing cottage just to the west, were covered by blown sand during the second half of the nineteenth century and only re-emerged during the late 1940s.

The ancient topography of the area around Green Shiel can be partially recreated through the production of a Digital Terrain Model (DTM) (**colour plate 3**). This is a three-dimensional, computer-generated map, based on points surveyed with an Electronic Distance Measurer (EDM). The reconstruction of the old land surface is made possible by test drilling down through the blown sand to trace the buried soil and the clay cliff. The heights and locations of these features are recorded as three-dimensional coordinates and these are used by the computer to develop the three-dimensional model. As the DTM illustrates, the area around Green Shiel was at one time devoid of dunes and the Anglo-Saxon site was located at the foot of a low clay cliff on top of which the agricultural soil developed.

Finally, the history of the Lindisfarne dune system is not complete without reference to rabbits, probably the most important influence after humans. This animal is a Norman introduction to England and was initially reared

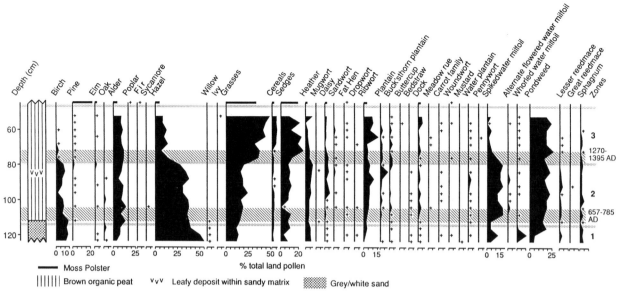

11 *Pollen diagram from the Lough, showing the fluctuations in vegetation type on Lindisfarne.*

as a controlled food resource, then allowed to run wild. It is not necessarily the pest that many assume it to be, as although it is often stated that rabbits have a destructive effect on dune vegetation this is only true if the rabbit population becomes too great and over-grazes a dune area, thus destabilizing it and allowing increased sand drifting. Rabbit populations of a certain size can stimulate an eco-system and increase vegetation diversity. A decrease in the rabbit population due to myxomatosis has sometimes resulted in the development of overgrown and impoverished dune areas.

The ecology of the island: a historical perspective

The exploitation of the local environment on Lindisfarne for economic purposes can best be considered in terms of the history of its farming and fishing. It might be assumed from some accounts of the island that farming did not emerge as an efficient and organized practice until the enclosure of the land in 1792–3. However, farming of some sort must have been carried out since before early medieval times. With the arrival of the Iona monks, the growing of crops and the rearing of domestic animals

would have reached a new period of intensification. It is well known that St Cuthbert, while living as a hermit on Farne, cultivated part of this island for his own requirements. Farming on Lindisfarne would obviously have been a more elaborate affair but unfortunately the sources provide no detail; documentary sources, however, do indicate that hemp, flax, onions, leeks and beans were all produced for the later Benedictine community although some of these may have been produced on the mainland. There is also evidence for the continued cultivation of cereals and grasses, probably for hay.

Throughout the history of farming on the island there has been a continued process of clearance of trees and shrubs and their replacement with cereals and grasses. The evidence for this is derived from the study of pollen from the Lough (**11**). Sediments in the bottom of many lakes gradually build up a sample of the pollen produced by local and regional flora over a period of time. A core taken from such a lake is a historical record of the pollen 'rain' for that area. By taking a sequence of samples from the core, and identifying the relative frequencies of different types of pollen, it is possible to develop a picture of how the flora in the area has changed over time.

The Lindisfarne pollen diagram reveals some very clear trends. Most important is the relative decline of trees and the associated increase in grasses: this is most obvious in the top zone of the diagram (zone 3), the beginning of this phase is radiocarbon dated to 1270–1395. Prior to this open landscape, the island had a different appearance: there must have been a reasonable area of hazel and birch woodland; this may have occupied the area south of the dunes, running into the modern-day arable area. Eventually these trees would have been cleared in order to make way for more intensive farming on the island. This clearance was certainly underway during the seventh century when the Anglo-Saxon monastery was first established: the beginning of zone 2 on the pollen diagram is known to be contemporary with this as it has been radiocarbon dated to 657–785.

The relatively high proportion of grasses and weeds associated with pasture, and the low proportion of cereals, implies that there has always been a greater emphasis on rearing animals than arable farming. The peak of cereal production probably took place during the nineteenth century, a period which saw an intensification of farming on the island, resulting from the enclosure of the land under the Enclosure of the Common Land Act in 1791–3 (see **79**). Relatively intensive farming has continued into the modern period, although the very top of the pollen diagram shows a decrease in cereals, indicating a slight move away from arable farming in recent times.

The seashore and fishing

As well as the exploitation of the island for farming, the shoreline would also have been an important economic resource. Certain livestock, especially sheep, could have been maintained on the shoreline by grazing on kelp and seaweed, a practice still common in some parts of Britain today. However, the most important resource would have been shellfish. On the shores of Lindisfarne there is a wide range

of shellfish, the different species occupying different types of shore environment. Lindisfarne is fortunate in that it possesses both expansive rocky platforms, and extensive sand and mud flats. On the rocky North Shore, for example, shellfish are plentiful, largely due to the flourishing seaweed and the limestone which provides them with the carbonate necessary for shell development. Here people will always have found plenty of limpets, whelks and winkles. There are mussels, but nowadays these never grow large enough to be worth collecting; once they reach a certain size they are washed away by the strong wave action on this shore. Elsewhere, on the extensive sandy shorelines, the burrowing shellfish are more common, the most important being the cockle.

This resource is also one that has been utilized for as long as humans have visited or inhabited the island. Prehistoric people are known to have valued shellfish, and it was probably also a useful resource during the early medieval period. Bede noted the abundance of shellfish, implying their significance to the Anglo-Saxon peoples. At the Green Shiel site, large quantities of the shells of limpets and winkles, as well as of mussels and whelks, have been found. However, shellfish were never a substantial part of any group's diet; it is far more likely that they were to serve as fishing bait. This may still have been the case during the later medieval period as the midden at Jenny Bell's Well, adjacent to the modern village, has also produced quantities of discarded shell. In the middle of the nineteenth century the collection of shellfish as bait for fishing was at its peak. As one visitor to the island noted:

> A stroll through the village disclosed very sensibly the nature of the principal occupation of the natives. In every street heaps of shells of the mussel and limpet are collected before the doors, and mixed with the refuse of the fishing lines... (G. Johnston 1854)

This leads us to consider the most valuable resource available to the islanders, the fish of the North Sea. Historically the islanders have fished for skate, cod, ling, lobster, haddock, herring and salmon, while today crab is very popular. The history of the fishing industry is considered in the last chapter. Most of the fishing done from the island has been inshore and even during the fishing fleet's heyday, the majority of fishing was done close to the island itself or around the Farne Islands. Herring and cod were especially important, with the majority of this catch coming from the waters around the Farnes.

The sand flats and bird-life

Most small islands support relatively limited floral and faunal communities: the diversity of species on an island tends to be lower than on an adjacent mainland. Also, certain species are over-represented, for example birds, which will obviously find it a lot easier to reach an island, will be far more successful than many mammals. Partly for this reason Lindisfarne has become famous for its bird populations. However, the most important reason for the presence of such large and varied populations of wildfowl, sea fowl and waders is the availability of plentiful supplies of food, the most important of which exist on the extensive sand and mud flats which almost surround the island.

It is a basic ecological rule that in coastal environments the number and variety of organisms increases as the grain size of the beach sediment decreases. For example, a rocky shore with boulders will only support marine molluscs (as mentioned earlier), crustaceans and a few other organisms. With finer sediments, such as gravels, sands, and then finally, the silts and muds, the richness of species increases. The number of burrowing animals, including a range of marine molluscs and worms becomes greater, as well as plant types such as the seagrasses (the *Spartina* species) and the eel-grasses (*Zostera*), which reach their peak on the finest sediments. As a consequence of this richness in both flora and fauna many birds are attracted to the rich feeding grounds.

As with the other environments already considered, there is little doubt that the flats around Lindisfarne have altered a great deal during the island's past. Sand and mud flats, and the species of flora found in them, are greatly affected by salinity, which is related to the level and frequency of tides in an area. Sea levels have never been stable, and as discussed earlier, those in this area have probably increased in relative terms, thus potentially enlarging the area of flats subject to salty conditions.

However, it is also possible for sea-level rises to be offset by increased sedimentation. The sand flats around Lindisfarne have certainly grown during the recent past as a result of the planting of cord grass (*Spartina townsendii*) which traps sediment washed in by the tides. Unfortunately, this grass also poses a threat to the main food supply of the Pale-bellied Brent Goose (*Branta bernicla*). This goose thrives on the eel-grass species which is an important constituent of any mud/sand flat or salt marsh environment.

The flats around Lindisfarne best reveal the complicated network of relationships that exist in all environments. They are a result of the balance between a wide range of natural processes: sea-level changes, sedimentation, the evolution of communities of sea and eel grasses, and the success of the various marine mollusc populations. All of these in turn support the various bird populations, from wildfowl such as the wigeon (the most common duck species that frequents the island), mallard, teal and mute swan, to the waders such as the oyster-catcher, dunlin, curlew, ringed plover and bar-tailed godwit. Human beings are at the very top of this network of relations.

Humans have undoubtedly always exploited the resources found on the sand and mud flats, whether it be for digging up bait for fishing, or perhaps the lucky taking of a bird before the advent of hunting guns. However, once the gun had been invented the human impact on many environments, including the sand flats of Lindisfarne, increased beyond all recognition – the most successful hunters were able to kill tens of birds with one shot.

Environmental damage and conservation

The exploitation of Lindisfarne starts in prehistory but the roots of the more recent intensification of exploitation go back to the nineteenth century. By the mid-twentieth century the different environments on the island were clearly suffering at human hands.

In the final chapter it will be shown how the island witnessed its own small-scale agricultural and industrial revolution in the eighteenth and nineteenth centuries. This resulted in a dramatic increase in the human population, which was itself a consequence of the more intense environmental exploitation. First came the intensification of agriculture as a result of enclosure. Secondly, during the 1840s the development of extractive industry transformed much of the north coast of the island. Thirdly, the fishing industry reached its peak at this time. As could only be expected, the combination of these factors led to a considerable pressure on available resources: wood and water, especially, would have been in great demand. The island would have probably seen the destruction of any remaining woodland; indeed a sycamore plantation on the east bank of the Lough was certainly partially removed in order to make way for a trackway to the limekilns near the castle. The reorganization of the landscape for more extensive agriculture would have had quite an impact on both the appearance and the ecology of Lindisfarne. It is likely that the uppermost and latest section of the pollen diagram corresponds with the beginning of this period, showing a decrease in tree pollen and an increase in grass pollen. The changes in tree and grass pollen imply the opening up of the landscape, with trees and shrubs making way for grasses associated with agriculture. Also, the decrease of spiked water milfoil, a species of plant which prefers still or slow fresh water may be indicative of an increase in the frequency of the Lough drying out. This in turn may be due to changes in the climate, or,

more likely, the consequence of an increased demand on fresh water on an island which lacks a plentiful supply of this most important of all natural resources. Of course, the inhabitants were simply continuing or repeating human actions which had been taking place for many centuries. There is no doubt, however, that this period would have seen many of the resources of the island stretched to extremes. The continued pressure of a relatively high population during the nineteenth century may have been more stressful for the island's ecosystem than the frequent, but short, intervals of tourist impact during recent years.

Growing awareness of environmental damage led to the establishment of the Lindisfarne National Nature Reserve in 1964. The reserve, comprising 260ha (647 acres) of sand and mud flats, and dune area, as well as the Lough, was largely established to protect wildfowl from over-hunting. The impact of tourism was also increasingly visible: the sand dune areas, especially fragile environments, required protection from vehicles and even careless walkers, who can do substantial damage to dune areas and cause destabilization.

Today, the nature reserve is managed on a day-to-day basis by the wardens of English Nature (formerly the Nature Conservancy Council). A large part of their responsibility lies in the control of wildfowling through the issue of permits and the monitoring of numbers killed. The wardens are also there to ensure that the reserve as a whole is not abused in any way, from watching for the unsanctioned use of vehicles in the dunes, to the removal of litter from around the reserve. The wardens also carry out, and assist, various environmental research projects; from studies of bird and rabbit populations, to research on the history of the sand dunes, work which is an invaluable contribution to the understanding and protection of one of Britain's most important coastal environments, one which has brought pleasure, as well as the necessities of life, to many generations in the past and, it is to be hoped, will continue to do so for many more.

3
Lindisfarne in prehistory

Given the richness of the archaeological remains of later periods that are visible on Lindisfarne it might come as a surprise to learn that the prehistoric period is the least well documented of the phases of human occupation on the island. Indeed, prior to the work of the authors over the last twelve years, the only prehistoric evidence known from the island consisted of a few isolated stray finds. Its proximity to the mainland made it seem unlikely that Lindisfarne had remained uninhabited throughout prehistory, but because of its small area, and also perhaps because of its Anglo-Saxon importance, no search for the remains of earlier times had been considered worthwhile.

12 Nessend Quarry from the south-west, showing exposed areas of boulder clay.

Nessend Quarry

This situation changed in the course of the preliminary survey of 1980, when the first prehistoric site was discovered. On the north side of the island, around the nineteenth-century limestone quarry at Nessend, there is an area of land which has seen considerable surface erosion (**12**). The dune and shallow vegetation cover has been completely removed in places and the underlying boulder clay exposed (**13**). It was here that we found a considerable scatter of struck flint and other worked stone lying on the surface of the boulder clay in several concentrations of various sizes. Initial fieldwork recovered some 381 pieces of flint and other worked stones, including some recognizable tool types as well as the cores from which flakes and blades had been removed.

A programme of detailed fieldwork was carried out at Nessend in the summers of 1983 and 1984. During this, a detailed record of the location of each piece of worked stone in the eroded area was made, with a view to trying to identify discrete areas of prehistoric activity. Concentrations of different types of material might reflect areas of food preparation or tool manufacture, for example. The whole of the eroded area was divided into grid squares of 10sq.m. These in turn were further subdivided into 1m squares which provided the basis for the collection of material, with the location of each piece of stone recovered recorded two-dimensionally. As they moved over the gridded

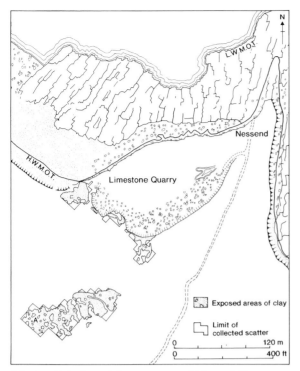

13 *Detailed plan of the area around Nessend Quarry, showing the extent of the exposed boulder clay and the area from which stone material was collected.*

area, each collector also produced a scale drawing of the areas of grass and small dune that they encountered. The end product was a very detailed map of the area, with each piece of struck stone precisely plotted. This was the first time that such a detailed approach to a lithic scatter had been adopted in north-east England. Over 2500 pieces were recovered and an initial analysis of the material showed that a long period of human activity on this part of Lindisfarne was involved.

The tool-types recovered included early and later Mesolithic microliths and petit-tranchet (transverse), leaf-shaped and barbed-and-tanged arrowheads of Neolithic and Bronze Age date, as well as blades, flakes, cores and modified flint and chert pebbles (**14**). Several bevelled pebbles, often referred to in the archaeological literature as 'limpet scoops', have also been found at Nessend. The raw material for these was mostly small flint pebbles,

but there were also examples of struck chert, quartz and chalcedony. These raw materials could have been obtained locally from the glacial till, although some may have been carried to the site from elsewhere. All of the stone used can be found in the river gravels of the Tweed which runs into the sea at Berwick to the north of the island.

The occurrence of so much stone material, ranging so widely in date in such a restricted area raises problems in its interpretation which relate both to the site itself and to further afield. A key question concerning the site itself was how the material had come to be there: most lithic scatters are discovered as a result of fieldwalking in ploughed fields, but there is now no soil cover at Nessend and no evidence that ploughing has ever taken place there. Given that the area is one which has obviously seen the development and erosion of sand dunes over time, the question of the processes of site formation that have been active at Nessend is a very interesting one. Is all of the material *in situ* or did it arrive at its present position on the boulder clay as the result of sand dunes blowing out, causing material deposited at different periods to come together on the eroded surface?

To try to answer this question two limited excavations were carried out on small sand dunes as part of the 1983 season of work. In the course of the excavations sand from the dunes was passed through a very fine mesh sieve, but no finds were recovered from the body of either dune. However, a few worked pieces were recovered from the interface between the sand and boulder clay in one area. That apart, no material which might help to date the dune formation was discovered, although evidence of earlier turf lines, indicating periods of dune stability, was recorded. On balance it seems that the lithic material represents several different periods of human activity in a 'preferred area'. As outlined in the previous chapter, the main dune system on Lindisfarne is probably of fairly recent origin;

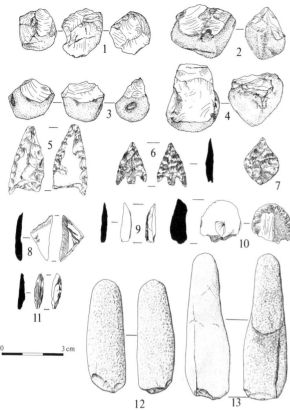

14 *Flint artefacts from Nessend. 1–4: cores; 5–7: arrowheads; 8,9,11: microliths; 10: scraper; 12–13: bevelled pebbles.*

'modified' pebbles (15 examples – 0.58% of the collection) is of interest. The latter are flint pebbles which have had only one flake removed from them before they have been discarded. This gives the impression that the prehistoric inhabitants of the area were highly selective of the raw materials from which they chose to make tools. All of the flint present at Nessend is in well-rolled pebble form. It may be that the site's primary function was as a source of raw materials and it was where tools were made. This might help to explain the lack of finished tools in the collection. Further support for this interpretation is given by the number of discarded cores that are present (86 complete examples and 26 shattered pieces, together making up 4.5% of the collection). The tools may subsequently have been used elsewhere.

The occurrence of microliths (13 examples) and bevelled pebbles at the site is also worthy of further comment. It is well known that the subsistence strategies of the Mesolithic period were firmly based on hunting/fishing and gathering. Several studies have suggested that Mesolithic groups were highly organized in terms of the way they exploited locally available resources, moving in a seasonally prescribed but planned round to exploit different food stuffs as and when they became available. The Mesolithic data from Nessend may be linked to these types of movement. The standard interpretation of microliths is that they were used to make composite, multi-piece, projectile weapons. It has also been suggested that far from being hammers or scoops for the removal of limpets from rocks, bevelled pebbles may have a close link with the working and cleaning of seal skins, acting as scraper-like tools for the removal of fat and flesh. In Wales, a possible correlation between the distribution of these implements and the known breeding grounds of seal has been noted, and if this is the case then their occurrence in the north-east coastal zone, with its known seal populations would not be out of place. The presence of later arrowhead forms may be due to the fact that

it is possible that earlier systems of coastal sand dunes may have formed in prehistoric times, but there is no way of demonstrating this on present evidence. The nature of early vegetation and soil cover at Nessend is therefore unclear.

Because of the nature of the assemblage it has not proved possible to realize our original aim of discovering the possible functions of different parts of the site. However, several general points can be made about the tasks which may have been carried out at Nessend in the various phases of the prehistoric period. Overall there is a very low proportion of finished tools from the site when compared with the evidence for generalized flint and stone knapping (44 examples – 1.7% of the total collection). In particular the number of unworked flint pebbles (49 examples – 1.9% of the collection) and what we have termed

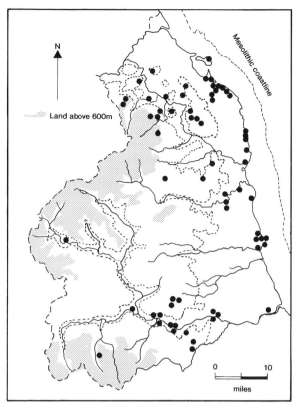

15 *The distribution of Mesolithic sites in Northumberland, showing the position of the Mesolithic coastline* (after J. Davies).

the Nessend area was also important as a hunting location at certain times in the Neolithic and Bronze Ages.

Of more wide-ranging interest is the relationship between the Nessend material and other stoneworking finds from the north-eastern coastal area. A number of flint scatters are known along the coasts of Durham and Northumberland. Francis Buckley, a noted northern prehistorian of the 1920s, recorded Mesolithic material from Spindleston, Budle Bay, Chester Crags and Ross Links, and Arthur Raistrick, another well-known northern archaeologist with interests as diverse as prehistory and industrial archaeology, collected and reported on similar finds from Newbiggin Point, Element Head, Sandle Holes and Lyne Hill in the 1930s. The material from these sites is very similar to that from Nessend. This early work has been supplemented most recently by local

fieldwork and an excavation on a coastal site at Low Hauxwell. The location of the Nessend site is comparable to that of scatters at Newbiggin and at Crimdon Dene on the Durham coast near Hartlepool.

The present surroundings of these sites give little clue to the appearance of the landscape in prehistoric times, however. The most recent work on the north-east coast indicates that there may have been two periods of coastal inundation starting in the early part of the post-glacial period. As discussed in the previous chapter, before these rises in sea level, the Mesolithic shoreline of north-east England would have lain much further to the east (see **15**). At the time of the earliest human activity on Lindisfarne the area would therefore not have been an island in any sense, and this observation has certain implications for the broader interpretation of both the Lindisfarne material and other so-called coastal lithic scatter sites. Lindisfarne would have been nothing more than a low hill in a flat, wooded landscape running back from the sea to the Cheviot Hills. Many other prehistoric sites have been lost as a result of rises in sea level. The site at Nessend may thus be an important survival of a much larger network of prehistoric sites and activity areas in this part of Northumberland.

Other prehistoric evidence from Lindisfarne

Other prehistoric archaeological material from the island is scarce. In 1936 Buckley found a single microlith in the area of the Castle Rock, and a fragment of a polished stone Neolithic axehead was found during the construction of the District Council car park in the 1960s. In 1979 Richard Coleman-Smith recovered a middle to late Bronze Age socketed spearhead from the shore at Jenny Bell's Well, to the southwest of the present village (**16**). The excavations at the midden site of Jenny Bell's Well in 1986 also recovered a few residual sherds of prehistoric pottery.

A further possible prehistoric feature can be

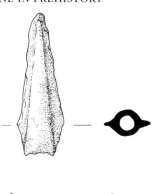

0 _____ 5 cms

16 *The Bronze Age spearhead from Jenny Bell's Well midden (after M. Hurrell).*

17 *The early midden eroding from the south-east end of the Heugh.*

seen beneath the fort at Steel End on the Heugh. Here, on the south coast of the island, a series of deposits is eroding from the cliff face as they are gradually being washed away by seasonal high tides. These deposits have been monitored since the mid-1980s and **17** and **18** show the stratigraphy of the material. Layers 5 and 7 are of particular interest: they are two of the earliest deposits on the Heugh, lying directly over the whin sill that makes up the cliff line. Small quantities of charcoal, struck flint, shell and sheep bones have been recovered from them. However, so far nothing has been recovered that would help us date the site directly.

There is no clear evidence of when farming

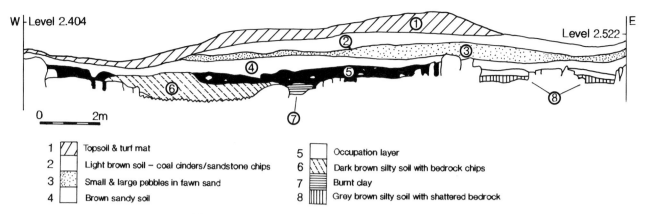

W ⊢Level 2.404

Level 2.522

0   2m

1	Topsoil & turf mat	5	Occupation layer
2	Light brown soil – coal cinders/sandstone chips	6	Dark brown silty soil with bedrock chips
3	Small & large pebbles in fawn sand	7	Burnt clay
4	Brown sandy soil	8	Grey brown silty soil with shattered bedrock

18 *Section drawing of the early midden on the Heugh.*

began on Lindisfarne itself. It is reasonable to suppose that Neolithic people would have gradually cleared the natural forest in the area and introduced a more settled way of life, but early prehistoric farming settlements are very difficult to identify. The axe head fragment is evidence for human activity on the island at this time; a number of Neolithic sites have been found in the Milfield basin, suggesting that pastoral farming was introduced into north Northumberland in the fourth millennium BC. We can likewise suppose that there may have been a later prehistoric community, but there is no real indication as yet of the whereabouts of the settlement, although one has been identified at Ross Links, on the mainland opposite the island.

Some Roman material has also been found on the island. The Jenny Bell's Well excavations produced a few abraded sherds of pottery and the museum also has in its collection some Roman pottery, including the encrusted neck of an amphora, thought to have come from a shipwreck somewhere in the vicinity of the present harbour.

The prehistoric archaeology of Lindisfarne may be difficult to find and visually it will never be as immediate or eye-catching as the archaeology of later periods. However, if we are to reach a full understanding of how the island has developed then it has an important place in our story.

4

The Golden Age:
the Anglo-Saxon monastery of
Lindisfarne

Early Northumbria

After the withdrawal of the Roman army at the beginning of the fifth century, northern Britain seems to have been divided into a number of independent kingdoms, with native British rulers. From the middle years of the fifth century the *Adventus Saxonum* – the 'Coming of the Saxons' also resulted in the establishment of a number of English kingdoms. Although there are some early accounts of the Anglo-Saxon invasions these are usually neither contemporary nor reliable, and the best evidence for the spread of the newcomers comes from the distinctive objects with which they were buried, which are found over most of southern and eastern England, including Yorkshire. There is not much early evidence of this type in Northumberland, but by the time proper historical sources emerge in the seventh and eighth centuries it is clear that there is Anglo-Saxon cultural and political hegemony all over England, and indeed in parts of what is now Scotland. In the seventh century the kingdom of Northumbria was the most powerful in the land, although this primacy was subsequently ceded to Mercia and then Wessex.

Very little is known for certain about the course of events which brought this about. It has been claimed that the Welsh poems attributed to the sixth-century bards Aneirin and Taliesin, which deal with the tradition of The Men of the North, preserve some account of the defeat in battle of the British at the hands

of the Anglo-Saxons. A number of encounters are described including a particularly heroic struggle at the battle of Catraeth (Catterick in north Yorkshire), probably in the latter part of the sixth century. However, these poems are increasingly being recognized as literary rather than historical creations. Although they may give some flavour of the times they are at least as likely to reflect a later preoccupation with a heroic past.

In both Welsh literature and in later Anglo-Saxon sources, it is clear that Northumbria had originally been divided into two separate units, Deira and Bernicia (see **1**). The two kingdoms were ruled by separate lineages, and were ultimately united in the course of the seventh century. Deira, the southern kingdom, stretched from the Humber to the Tees. Bernicia extended from the Tees into much of lowland Scotland, and as far as the Forth for a limited period. The names of some of the post-Roman kingdoms of the north are known to us: there is a general consensus that the kingdom of Rheged covered most of Cumbria and south-west Scotland, while that of Strathclyde was north of this, around the Firth of Clyde. To the east was the kingdom of the Gododdin, around the Firth of Forth, and to the south, in the Leeds area, the kingdom of Elmet. The names of any independent British kingdoms along the east coast have not survived. However, Deira and Bernicia are actually names of British origin, and they may represent earlier political entities, which were simply taken over by Anglo-Saxon rulers.

An early Anglo-Saxon fortress?

Lindisfarne is first mentioned in connection with events of the late sixth century, in the group of documents known as the *Historia Brittonum*, attributed to the monk Nennius. This was apparently compiled at the beginning of the ninth century. It is a miscellaneous collection, whose value as a source of history has been seriously challenged. The notice of the island occurs in that part of it known as the *Northern History*. The document was compiled long after the events with which it is supposed to deal, and the source of Nennius' information about Northumbria is unclear. It is possible that the compiler had access to some early sources which have not survived. However, there is no evidence of history writing in Northumbria as early as the sixth century and it is uncertain what form any such early source might have taken, or how reliable it might have been.

The *Northern History* contains short notices of the Anglo-Saxon and British kings of northern Britain, and is clearly written from a British, rather than an Anglo-Saxon, viewpoint. The events on Lindisfarne follow on from a list of the regnal lengths of the sons of the Anglian king Ida, who has previously been attributed with unification of the two early Northumbrian kingdoms of Deira and Bernicia. It is then stated that

> …four kings fought against them, Urien, and Rhydderch Hen, and Gwallawg and Morcant. Theodoric fought vigorously against Urien and his sons. During that time, sometimes the enemy, sometimes the Cymry were victorious, and Urien blockaded them for three days and three nights in the island of Lindisfarne. But during this campaign, Urien was assassinated on the instigation of Morcant, from jealousy, because his military skill and generalship surpassed that of all the other kings…

The text then continues with an account of the reign of Aethelfrith. The logical assumption is that the events on Lindisfarne took place during the reign of Theodoric (*c.* 572–9), and before that of Aethelfrith (592–616).

This passage has been minutely dissected by historians who have allowed some authority to Nennius, as it offers key evidence for the relatively late and small-scale nature of Anglo-Saxon settlement in Northumberland. Urien, the murdered leader, is the subject of some of the Taliesin poems, where he is described as Urien of Rheged. Rhydderch Hen is likewise identified as a king of Strathclyde. It is possible that Nennius or his source simply selected these figures because they were already famous in song and story.

The Anglo-Saxon toehold in Bernicia was not particularly strong, even as late as the end of the sixth century. They occupied a number of naturally defensible coastal fortlets but with possibly some hinterland along the coast. If any reliance is to be placed on Nennius' text (and there are many who would not do so) then it is reasonable to infer that there was an early Anglo-Saxon fortress on Lindisfarne, perhaps comparable to that at Bamburgh. There are two possible sites for such a fortress: Biblaw, the pinnacle on which the castle now stands, and the Heugh. Naturally fortified places are frequently reused for defences of different periods, and the former is perhaps the more probable site. Resistivity survey (see **26**) hints at a possible enclosing wall around the top of the Heugh, but there is nothing to date this feature, and no early finds from either place. One way or another the island was clearly in royal hands when it was given to St Aidan, as the base from which the pagan Northumbrians would be converted to Christianity, in 635.

The foundation of the monastery

The story of Aidan's mission has been told many times. It was not the first attempt to introduce Christianity to northern England: in 625, Paulinus, a follower of St Augustine, had

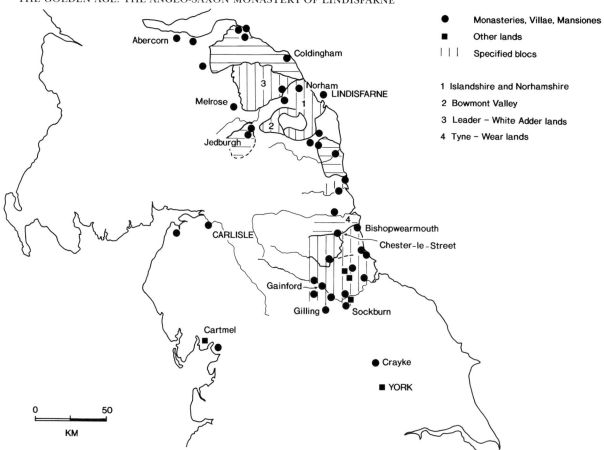

19 *The Northumbrian landholdings of the Community of St Cuthbert (after C.D. Morris).*

come from Canterbury with that very purpose. He came as part of the retinue of Princess Ethelberga of Kent, on the occasion of her marriage to King Edwin of Northumbria. Edwin accepted conversion in 627, but Paulinus' mission collapsed on the death of Edwin in 633 and he returned south.

Shortly after his accession to the throne, Edwin's successor, the Christian King Oswald, sent to Iona, the principal monastery of the Christian Scottish kingdom of Dalriada, for someone to act as the spiritual leader of his new kingdom. The first candidate for the job was of 'austere disposition' and his brief mission was unsuccessful. On his return to Iona, Aidan was chosen in his stead, a man 'particularly endowed with the grace of discretion'. Bede paints a glowing picture of Aidan's many virtues: his generosity and love of poverty, his devotion to the study of the Scriptures, and his personal austerity and dislike of ostentation. He clearly enjoyed an excellent relationship with Oswald who translated Aidan's preaching for his English audience. Oswald had spent his youth among the Irish and Scots and spoke their language fluently.

The king would certainly have endowed his new project with lands and other benefits. While there are no contemporary records of the extent of these, it is probable that the two estates later known as Islandshire and Norhamshire formed the core of this endowment, adjacent to his own royal estate of Bamburgh (**19** and see **76**). Personal gifts of valuable objects would also have been made: Bede describes the gift of a horse from Oswald's successor, Oswine, which Aidan immediately gave away to a beggar. The founder clearly embraced personal poverty, and Bede comments on the simplicity of the monastery in his time. This restraint was not necessarily seen as desirable by some of his successors, particularly where endowments to the monastery itself were concerned.

Lindisfarne was clearly originally founded as a daughter house of Iona, and the links between the two monasteries were initially very close. Aidan's immediate successors as Abbot and Bishop of Lindisfarne, Finan and Colman, were sent directly from Iona, rather than selected from the Lindisfarne community itself, and the abbots of Iona maintained a direct interest in the running of the monastery. During the abbacy of Colman, however, a controversy within the Northumbrian Church resulted in the severance of these close ties.

The controversy was principally about the date of the celebration of Easter: the Lindisfarne church, following the example of Iona, continued to use an elaborate early form of computation which was replaced in Rome in the sixth century by a simpler method, based on a twenty-nine-year cycle. Another matter of dispute was the correct form of clerical tonsure, the distinctive haircut worn by monks to distinguish them from lay people. Roman practice required that a circular area on the crown of the head be shorn off, whereas in Celtic areas, the usual custom was to shave the hair in a semi-circular arc, immediately back from the forehead. The church at Canterbury which had been established as the primatial see by St Augustine, conformed to the Roman practice. The specific issues may seem trivial today, but for contemporaries the whole question of conformity to the norms of the Universal Church, and the authority of the Pope at Rome to dictate these norms, was at stake. In the middle years of the seventh century a 'Romanizing' faction developed in Northumbria, led by Wilfrid of Hexham, which was determined to bring all of the Northumbrian Church into line with Roman practice. The Lindisfarne community felt that it was disrespectful to their own

tradition to alter the practice which they had inherited. The story of the dispute is given great prominence by the Venerable Bede in his Ecclesiastical History, who was in no doubt about its wider significance. A synod was held at the monastery of Whitby in 664 at which King Oswiu decided to cast his lot behind the Roman party. As a result, Colman decided to leave England for Ireland in disgust, taking with him those of the Lindisfarne brethren who refused to conform with the verdict of the synod. Colman was succeeded as Bishop of the Northumbrians by Tuda, an Irishman who conformed with the Roman practice. Eata, then Abbot of Melrose and one of Aidan's first English converts, became the new Abbot of Lindisfarne. Bede gives the impression that links with Iona were severed at this point, but Iona still seems to have kept an interest in the Northumbrian Church: Adamnan, Columba's biographer, made at least two 'official' visits to Northumbria during his abbacy in the early eighth century. It is perhaps significant that it was only during Adamnan's abbacy that the monks of Iona eventually conformed to the Roman Easter, in 715.

The career of Cuthbert, the most famous Prior and Bishop of Lindisfarne, is considered in the next chapter. Because of Cuthbert's 'high profile' in contemporary sources we know a reasonable amount about the history of Lindisfarne in the seventh and early eighth century, but for the late eighth and ninth centuries there is much less contemporary information about the internal history of the monastery. However, documents preserved by the community and incorporated into later histories written at Chester-le-Street and Durham provide evidence that it received generous endowments, usually in the name of Cuthbert. The Northumbrian king, Ceolwulf, became a monk of Lindisfarne on his retirement from the throne in 737, so the close links with royalty were to some extent maintained.

The poem De Abbatibus, from which the description of Lindisfarne quoted in the introduction is taken, was written at a cell of Lindisfarne in the early ninth century. It offers some insight into monastic practice, interests and values at this time. The standard of learning was high: its author, Aethelwulf, shows a knowledge of Latin authors such as Virgil and Ovid as well as the works of his English predecessors and contemporaries Aldhelm, Bede and Alcuin. He seems also to have had a practical interest in astronomy, and is knowledgeable about the history of his own monastery and its inmates, writing of the skill of the Irish scribe Ultan, and the musical interests of the fifth abbot, Sigwine. The precious treasures of his community are held in high regard, and there are a number of other indications that the monastery no longer aspired to the ascetic ideals of Aidan and Cuthbert. One of the monks whom Aethelwulf discusses may have been married, and this and other sources suggest that feasting, imbibing and the wearing of rich apparel had become the norm.

The Viking raids and the later history of the monastery

On 8 June, 793, Lindisfarne was once more thrust on to the centre stage:

Lo it is nearly 350 years that we and our fathers have inhabited this most lovely land, and never before has such terror appeared in Britain as we have now suffered from a pagan race, nor was it thought that such an inroad from the sea could be made. Behold the church of St Cuthbert spattered with the blood of the priests of God, despoiled of its ornaments. A place more venerable than all in Britain is given as prey to pagan peoples. And where, after the departure of St Paulinus from York, the Christian religion in our race took its rise, there misery and calamity have begun;...foxes pillage the chosen vine...

Thus wrote the scholar Alcuin of York, in a commiserating letter to the Northumbrian king. In another letter, to Higbald, Bishop of Lindisfarne, he writes

The calamity of your tribulation saddens me every day, though I am absent. When the pagans desecrated the sanctuaries of God, and poured out the blood of saints around the altar, laid waste the house of our hope, trampled on the bodies of saints in the Temple of God, like dung in the street...what assurance is there for the churches of Britain, if St Cuthbert, with so great a number of saints, defends not his own?...

In the *Anglo-Saxon Chronicle*, the same event is described as follows:

793: In this year terrible portents appeared over Northumbria, and miserably frightened the inhabitants: these were exceptional flashes of lightning, and fiery dragons were seen flying in the air. A great famine soon followed these signs; and a little after that in the same year on 8 June the harrying of the heathen miserably destroyed God's church on Lindisfarne by rapine and slaughter.

The Irish Annals of Ulster record the devastation of 'the islands of Britain' for the same year.

The raid on Lindisfarne was the first documented attack by Viking pirates on the west, and it obviously made a dramatic impact on contemporary writers. From the Anglo-Saxon viewpoint the raid came, quite literally, out of the blue. His writing draws partly on Old Testament parallels and imagery, but Alcuin clearly saw it as a sign of the anger of God at the sinful ways into which the Northumbrians had fallen. The passage quoted also indicates his shock that even the power of their great saint, Cuthbert, was no protection.

From the point of view of the Viking raiders, however, the attack was carefully planned. The wealth of the monastery was well known throughout the west, but also its unprotected location, even such factors as its shallow harbour, were all taken into account; the raiders had done their homework. Much discussion has taken place among scholars in the last few decades about the nature of Viking activity, and there is some consensus that the physical havoc wrought by the Vikings has been overstated, not least because the contemporary chroniclers and historians were all clerics, and most of the raids and rapine were carried out against churches and monasteries.

The period of raiding continued for four or five decades, but major attacks on important sites were not particularly frequent. Nonetheless,

the island and coastal monasteries were particularly vulnerable: the monastery of *Rechru*, also on a small, inshore island, usually identified with Lambay, off the north Dublin coast, was the scene of the first attack on an Irish monastery, in 794, and attacks soon followed on Jarrow (795) and Iona (795). The community of Columba left Iona at the beginning of the ninth century, relocating at the less vulnerable inland site of Kells. In the first half of the ninth century Viking activity seems to have been mostly concentrated against Ireland, and we hear of no further attacks on the north-east coast. However, the invasion of Northumbria by the Great Army and the

20 *The journeys of St Cuthbert's relics in the ninth and tenth centuries, and major Roman roads in the north (after D. Rolleson).*

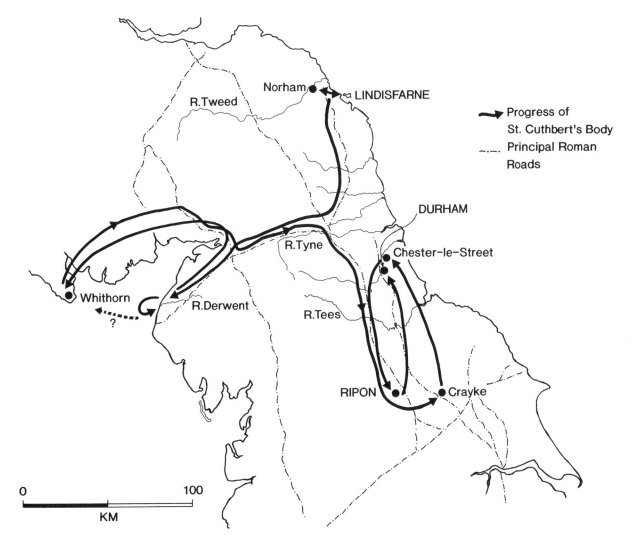

establishment of the Viking kingdom of York in 867 radically altered the political structure of north-east England, and sounded the end of the Golden Age: all of the major monasteries of the Northumberland coast seem to have been deserted in the course of the ninth century.

The Cuthbert community hung on for just over eighty years. In the time of Bishop Ecgred (830–45) they moved for a time to Norham-on-Tweed, selecting a site that was already part of their own endowment of land, but in a less vulnerable location. As well as the shrine of Cuthbert they took with them the bones of King Ceolwulf and the original wooden church built by Aidan on Lindisfarne, and re-erected it at Norham.

There was another attack on Lindisfarne in 875, which proved decisive. The monks decided to abandon their monastery, and, carefully packing up their most precious treasures, they set off on what proved to be an eight-year trek around the north of England, finally settling in Chester-le-Street in 883 (**20**). The shrine of Cuthbert accompanied them on these travels, as well as the head of St Oswald, the bones of Aidan and those of Bishops Eadberht, Eadfrith and Aethelwold, and, apparently, the stone cross of Aethelwold. Their original intention seems to have been to sail for Ireland: they travelled first through Cumbria to the mouth of the Derwent and embarked, but Cuthbert showed his disapproval of this course of action by turning waves into blood, so they changed course and went north to Whithorn. From Whithorn they went to Crayke in Yorkshire and from there to Chester-le-Street.

These travels may give the impression of rather unfocused wanderings, but in fact the community seems to have usually stayed at places which were already part of its own estates (see **19**) and it continued to build up its possessions in the tenth century, laying the foundations of the great landholdings of the later medieval 'prince-bishops' of Durham. It certainly never relinquished its estates north of the Tyne: these formed the kernel of the terri-

tory known as North Durham, a group of parishes incorporating the estates of Islandshire and Norhamshire which remained part of the diocese of Durham into modern times.

The monastic plan

The evidence for the physical layout of the monastery and the type of buildings used is meagre. Bede and the author of the anonymous *Life of Cuthbert* provide some incidental information, but they had little interest in describing the unremarkable, everyday surroundings of their own lives. Our reconstruction of the monastery (**colour plate 4**) is largely conjectural, and pieced together from a number of different sources, which include surviving remains, stray finds, place-names and later maps, and the fruits of archaeological investigation. We have also the benefits offered by comparable sites elsewhere.

Aidan would have brought with him his own perception of what a monastery should look like, and it is probable that his foundation in its initial years was modelled on Iona. His choice of the island is itself surely a reflection of this, as there are many points of topographical similarity (**21**). The two islands are of comparable size, and both have an open treeless landscape, with a restricted area of pasture and arable and some uncultivated waste in the northern part of the island. The early monasteries were also focused in both cases around a broad, shallow harbour. The most notable difference is that Iona is a 'true' island, which can only be reached by boat, although it is within clear site of land.

The most conspicuous early Christian feature in the landscape on Iona is a large D-shaped enclosure bank, which survives partly as an earthwork but can partly only be detected by geophysical methods (**21a**). This can be identified with the *vallum monasterii*, a bank and ditch which surrounded the monastic complex, mentioned by Adamnan in his *Life of Columba*.

On Lindisfarne there is nothing which is easily recognizable as a monastic vallum, even

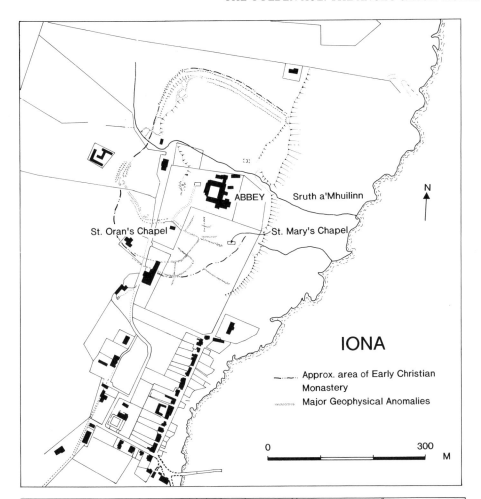

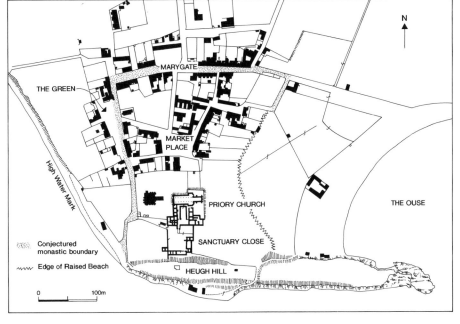

21 *Plan of the early Christian enclosure on Iona, and the suggested enclosure on Lindisfarne. The suggested enclosure on Lindisfarne is of comparable dimensions and aspects to that on Iona (after RCHM).*

from the air, and it could be argued that the need to enclose the monastic community and mark off the sacred from the secular, was not a vital aspect of the monastery here: this function possibly being fulfilled by the tides. However, when the street plan of the village is studied (21b), it is possible to identify at least part of a curvilinear boundary, surrounding the churchyard and the Benedictine priory. The monastery would have been delimited by natural features to the south and east – to the south by the Heugh, and to the east by the line of the raised beach which marks the earlier extent of the harbour. There are two possibilities for the northern boundary: one would be through the market place, which is linked to east and west by a continuous frontage, running from the raised beach to the road which runs past the west end of the parish church to the shore opposite St Cuthbert's Island. Alternatively, the line of the street known as Marygate also connects with these two features and would provide a substantially larger enclosure, comparable with that on Iona. Both boundaries may be significant: many early Christian Irish monastic sites have a small curvilinear enclosure surrounded by a larger one, and the possible existence of comparable features on Lindisfarne reinforces its early links with the Irish monastic tradition.

Contemporary historical sources refer to at least two churches on Lindisfarne, a small timber edifice built by Aidan, and a later church erected by Finan and dedicated to St Peter, which was also made of timber, although Bede states that later Bishop Eadberht (688–98) 'removed the thatch, and covered both roof and walls with sheets of lead'. This church contained the bones of Aidan, to the right side of the altar, and later the shrine of Cuthbert, also to the right of the altar. Other buildings specifically mentioned include a watchtower, a guesthouse and a dormitory, but there is no indication of the way in which these different buildings were arranged within the monastic precinct. It is probable that they were usually

made of wood; when the monastery was abandoned these would have rapidly decayed, leaving no visible trace above ground.

St Cuthbert's Island

It is clear from the early sources that the little island known now as St Cuthbert's Island (**colour plate 1**) but officially as Hobthrush or Thrush Island had a specific role in the spiritual life of the community. Initially it was used by Cuthbert and his successor Eadberht as a temporary solitary retreat. Bede observes that when St Cuthbert's incorrupt body was discovered

> At that time he [Eadberht] was living alone at some distance from the church in a place surrounded by the sea, where he always used to spend Lent and the forty days before the Nativity of Our Lord in fasting, prayer and penitence. It was here that his predecessor, Cuthbert had served God in solitude for a period before he went to Farne Island (Bede, *Historia Ecclesiastica* IV, 30).

Bede elsewhere describes St Cuthbert's retreat as being 'in the outer precincts of the monastery' (*Vita Cuthberti* XVII).

The early sources give no clue to the type of buildings on St Cuthbert's Island. However, the construction of the buildings of his retreat on Farne is described in some detail, and this may give us some idea of the kinds of structures to expect (**colour plate 5**). The saint built himself a circular enclosure of turf and locally quarried, unmortared stone, the floor of which was cut out of the living rock. Bede comments on the massive size of the stones used. In addition to his cell or dwelling-hut there was an oratory, and both buildings were roofed with timber and thatch. Cuthbert asked monks from Lindisfarne to provide him with structural timbers to build a floor for his cell, but when they forgot his request he made use of a large plank which turned up as flotsam. At a little distance from his cell, by the landing place 'there was a larger house in which the brethren

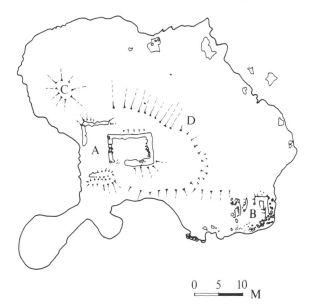

22 *Plan of the remains on St Cuthbert's Island, 1987.*

who visited him could be received and rest, and not far away was a well for their use' (Bede, *Vita Cuthberti* XVII). There was another well by his cell.

If arrangements on Farne offer any insight, it is reasonable to propose that the retreat on St Cuthbert's Island might have likewise consisted of a cell and an oratory, and possibly an enclosure. Given the proximity of the main monastery there would have been no need for a guesthouse, and possibly even a source of fresh water could have been dispensed with, although it would seem that Eadberht, and presumably Cuthbert before him, sought solitude here for fairly long periods. It is clear that in spite of regular visitors Cuthbert attempted a self-sufficient lifestyle on Farne, trying to grow his own crops of wheat and barley and relying on locally available building materials for the construction of his cell. However, the area of St Cuthbert's Island above the high-watermark is small (less than an acre) and it is also very windy and exposed. Unlike Farne, the island is also very easily accessible from the mainland and it would have been a simple matter to provide sustenance for anyone on retreat there from the resources of the main monastery.

Although the archaeological remains are scheduled St Cuthbert's Island is not in state care and no excavation has been attempted there since Crossman's work in the nineteenth century, already briefly described in the introduction. As part of the recent programme a resistivity survey of the island was carried out in 1987, but this failed to reveal any previously unknown archaeological evidence, and at least one of the features which he describes, the 'ancient walling' south-east of the chapel, close to the high-watermark, can no longer be seen (**22**). Virtually all of the visible remains must post-date the Anglo-Saxon monastery, but it has recently been suggested by Cramp that the 'breakwater' which Crossman identified surrounding the chapel may be the remains of an early enclosure. The medieval chapel may have obliterated the site of a previous oratory, but perhaps a more promising feature is the low mound to the north of the chapel and breakwater, planned but not discussed by Crossman, which could be the remains of a small circular cell of the type which is commonly found in the early Christian monastic sites of the western seaboard of Ireland. Only excavation is likely to clarify if this or any other structure dates from the time of Cuthbert.

The churches of Lindisfarne
Two medieval churches stand on Lindisfarne today, and it is possible to make some links between these buildings and the early monastery, although they are not necessarily the direct successors of the two timber churches mentioned by Bede. When the priory was refounded in the eleventh century, the priory church would have been constructed over the presumed site of St Cuthbert's shrine; in the later Middle Ages this was marked by a cenotaph. During early twentieth-century clearance a foundation was discovered underlying the north aisle wall, which 'belonged to a plain rectangular building, whose east wall was a little to the west of the east end of this aisle'. This was clearly a stone foundation, but it

arch are visible. Above this is a rectangular doorway, and the line of an earlier roof (**23**). This earlier roofline is clearly itself later than the round arch and the doorway, so these two features must come from a church at least two stages of development earlier than the existing one. The round-headed arch and the doorway are not easy to date, but they could be of the Anglo-Saxon period. Likewise, outside, on the north side of the building at the junction of the nave and chancel with the north aisle, there is a line of irregular, squared blocks in the east wall of the nave which indicates an earlier north-east corner (**24**). This type of masonry, or quoining, is also not closely datable, but it could be Anglo-Saxon work. Seen from both inside and outside, therefore, the east wall of

24 *Irregular quoining in the exterior face of the east wall of the nave.*

23 *Walling above the west face of the chancel arch in St Mary's church, Lindisfarne showing the line of an earlier arch and opening.*

could still have formed part of Finan and later Bishop Eadberht's church of St Peter (referred to above) if this had been rebuilt in stone in the eighth or ninth century.

Immediately west of the priory church is the parish church of St Mary, which is for the most part a building of the thirteenth century (see below, Chapter 9). A careful examination of the church fabric reveals a number of features which belong to an earlier structure which lies at its core, however.

Inside the church, above the present pointed chancel arch the remains of an earlier, rounded

25 *The Heugh, from the shore.*

the nave would appear to belong to an earlier, and possibly Anglo-Saxon, stone church.

Such a stone church would clearly not date from the earliest phase of the monastery, when even the principal church was built in timber. Later, when the community became subject to different influences, however, the construction of impressive masonry buildings may have become more acceptable. The location of the church, immediately due west of the probable site of the principal church of St Peter, raises the possibility that there was an axial arrangement of Anglo-Saxon churches. This is something which is also found at the fellow Northumbrian monasteries of Hexham and Jarrow, and it is perhaps an indication of the influence of these centres. Alternatively, the earlier stone

church may have been built in the tenth or eleventh century to serve the needs of the local community: there is a noticeable difference in the east–west orientation of the churches, which might be explained by the passage of time.

There is some further late evidence for another church on Lindisfarne: a priory document of 1395 makes reference to the churchyard of St Columb. The exact whereabouts of this are not precisely known, but it seems to have been on the north side of the village, somewhere between Lewin's Lane and the main road to Berwick. The dedication to Columba reinforces the link with Iona, but the origins of the chapel are unknown. It is possibly the site of an early burial ground. Columba is also commemorated in St Coomb's Farm, a now ruinous group of farm buildings on the Straight Lonnen. A number of burials have been found east of the

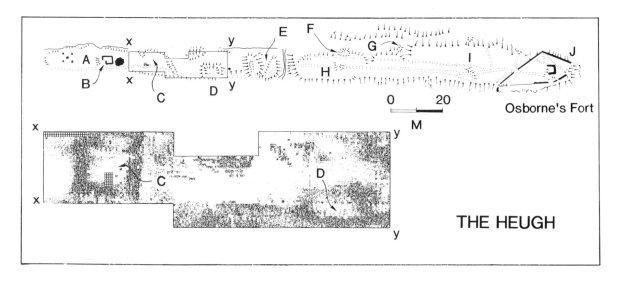

26 *Survey of the Heugh, showing a low, curved mound (A); the ruin known as the chapel (B); ?watchtower foundations (C); small rectangular buildings (D,F,G,H); the 'Cockpit' (E); a curved bank (I); and Osbourne's Fort (J).*

presumed site of this churchyard, suggesting that there must have been a number of early graveyards, perhaps maintaining a distinction between secular and monastic interments.

The excavation on the site of the museum in 1977 produced two early features – an area of small limestone paving and a shallow hearth – which were probably part of another structure. There was no associated dating evidence, but a period of abandonment clearly followed, before the site was used again in the later medieval period. The features may have been part of the interior of an early Christian monastic building, the rest of which had been obliterated by later pits and other features; alternatively, it could be of even earlier date.

The buildings on the Heugh

Other archaeological remains near the priory have no known history but are also possibly connected with the early monastery. Along the Heugh (**25, 26**), is a series of small, shallow ruins only clearly visible in late spring when the growth of grass is at its lowest. As noted in the

introduction, some of them were first observed in the late nineteenth century by a casual visitor to the island, and at least one was excavated by Brian Hope-Taylor in the 1960s. The visible features were surveyed by the Lindisfarne Research Project in 1984–5, and a resistivity survey of the whole ridge was also carried out, to see if further evidence existed below ground.

At the western end of the Heugh, just west of the early modern ruin known as the 'chapel', is a low curved mound (A on **26**), maybe simply rubble from the 'chapel'. However, features to the east of this have a more recognizable plan and a more justifiable claim to some antiquity. Just to the east of the present war-memorial is a low mound (C), which resistivity survey suggests is part of a building foundation approximately 15m (50ft) square, from which a pathway worn through the rock runs down the north side of the Heugh towards the priory. Further east, at D, the foundations of a small rectangular building, oriented east–west, are clearly visible. To the east of this again, straddling the centre of the ridge, is a circular mound known as the Cock-pit. A rectangular trench has been cut in this since Blackwell first observed it, probably during the First World War. On the top is a stone cross-base.

To the east of the path which bisects the Heugh a number of other shallow foundations of small rectangular buildings can be seen. Two of these at F and G were partly explored by Hope-Taylor and are aligned east–west. Another, at H, seems to run north–south across the ridge, while further along, at I, a curved bank may form part of another rather larger east–west building.

Without excavation it is only possible to speculate on the purpose of this series of structures, but they have no obvious place in the arrangements of the medieval priory or the medieval or early modern village. In Bede's account of the death of Cuthbert, he makes explicit reference to a watchtower, from which one of the Lindisfarne monks watched for news of Cuthbert's death. When the saint died, those attending him lit two torches, as a prearranged signal that he had passed away, and the monk 'quickly ran to the church where the whole of the brethren were assembled'. Excellent views of Inner Farne can be obtained from the Heugh, and it is possible that one of the small buildings served the function of a watchtower. Other structures may have served as small chapels or retreats, more in the pattern of a dispersed, Irish-type of monastic complex. They may have been 'stations', shrines or stages in a circuit of the monastic precinct associated with a devotional ritual of pilgrimage, known in early Christian Ireland as a *turas*. There is some indirect evidence for such a pilgrimage route in one of the miracle stories connected with St Cuthbert's relics. The features on the Heugh and the scattered nature of the early churches and cemeteries is certainly paralleled at Iona, where a church of the eighth century has just been discovered underlying the later medieval church of St Ronan, about 1km (¾ mile) south of the abbey.

The Anglo-Saxon stone carvings
The English Heritage museum on Lindisfarne contains a substantial collection of Anglo-Saxon stone carvings, many in a fragmentary condition. Although the precise findspots of the carvings are not always known, they seem to have been mostly found in or about the later Benedictine priory; one was found on St Cuthbert's Island. The carvings are of different types, and date from the eighth, ninth and tenth centuries and they are all of great interest.

The earliest group includes a number of small, flat stones known as 'namestones', decorated with crosses and short inscriptions which were probably placed on individual graves (**27** a, b). The names include at least one woman, Osgyth. A number of similar stones come from the site of the contemporary monastery at Hartlepool, which was also founded under the influence of Aidan, and examples are also known from Monkwearmouth and Billingham.

The best-known of all of the Lindisfarne sculptures is the so-called Warrior Stone – a slab with a rounded top and carving on both sides (**28**). One face shows a procession of warriors; on the reverse are symbols of the sun and moon, and two kneeling figures with hands upraised, placed on either side of a cross. Hands

27a,b Lindisfarne name stones (English Heritage).

28 *The Warrior Stone* (English Heritage).

is surprisingly little evidence for high-quality stone-carving, such as might be expected from the monastery which produced the Lindisfarne Gospels. The most impressive early Anglo-Saxon sculptures are from other Northumbrian monasteries, outside the influence of Lindisfarne, such as Wearmouth and Jarrow. It would appear that a tradition of fine stone-carving never developed on the island during the Golden Age. One cross-shaft fragment is carved with some interlaced animals which have on occasion been compared with the patterns of the Lindisfarne Gospels (29), but the majority of the surviving carvings actually date from the period after the abandonment of the Anglo-Saxon monastery. One of these later shafts shows a seated figure with a halo enclosed within a roundel and surrounded by figures with trumpets and books above a panel of interlace. This is probably a depiction of Christ

29 *Cross shaft with interlaced animals* (English Heritage).

reach from the side of the stone towards the arms of the cross. The procession of warriors has sometimes been taken as a depiction of Viking raiders, but the art of the period did not usually simply depict contemporary reality and the stone is currently thought to convey images of Doomsday, as described in the Scriptures.

Many of the carved stones are fragments of high crosses which would once have stood in the monastic precinct. According to later sources, Bishop Aethelwold had a stone high cross carved in honour of St Cuthbert in about 740, which may have been the first large stone monument. Most of the buildings of the monastery at this stage were probably still made of wood, and among the sculptures there on Judgement Day, surrounded by angels (**30**). Most of the others are decorated with panels of interlace and animal ornament. These are often fairly crude sculptures, but they provide important evidence for a religious presence on the island, and also probably indicate the continuous use and maintenance of the monastic burial ground, though possibly for secular purposes.

30 *Cross shaft showing Christ in Judgement* (English Heritage).

5

The Golden Age: St Cuthbert and Lindisfarne

In 698, eleven years after the death of Cuthbert, perhaps their most devout and celebrated prior and bishop, the monks of Lindisfarne decided to move his bones from their original burial place in a stone sarcophagus at the right of the altar in the Church of St Peter, to a new coffin, a 'light chest' which would be kept above ground in the same place. When the original coffin was opened, to the wonderment of all present, the body inside was found to be miraculously preserved. This was seen as a direct indication from God of Cuthbert's power and sanctity, and a shrine was constructed over his second grave, which became the focus of a major cult. Cuthbert rapidly rose to pre-eminence among the saints of Northumberland, and within a generation of his death he was venerated all over the north of England.

The cult of Cuthbert surrounded his physical body and tomb. This was seen as a place of miracles; elaborate ceremonies took place on his feast-day and the shrine was adorned with rich gifts and offerings. There was little precedent for this kind of cult in England, and it seems also to have been foreign to the tradition of Iona. Scholars now believe that the inspiration for the cult probably came from Gaul, where many of these features find echoes in rituals and cults surrounding a number of Merovingian saints: the uncorrupted body, the movement or 'translation' to an elaborate tomb, and the occurrence of many miracles at the site of the tomb.

Among the products of the new cult was a life of the saint, written by a monk of the Lindisfarne community and known as the *Anonymous Life of St Cuthbert*. This is one of the earliest surviving accounts of a saint's life from the British Isles, and was probably written about 700, less than a generation after his death. Making use of this early account and also of his personal knowledge and contacts, the Venerable Bede wrote two lives of St Cuthbert at the invitation of the Lindisfarne community in the early eighth century, one in conventional Latin prose, another in verse. These texts are our principal sources for Cuthbert's own life, but it is important to remember that their aim was very different from that of modern biography. Their main function was to show the workings of God through the life and deeds of his servant Cuthbert, and their focus was devotional and moral rather than strictly historical. They recount a series of events in the life of the saint, often of a marvellous or miraculous nature, and not necessarily in strict chronological order. They also show clear knowledge of some of the Gaulish saints' lives on which they are in part modelled, especially that of St Martin of Tours by Sulpicius Severus. The Life of Cuthbert was a popular devotional work throughout the Middle Ages, and a number of later, illustrated versions exist.

Nothing is known of Cuthbert's parentage but from the age of eight it is recorded that he

31 *Twelfth-century illustrations of the Life of St Cuthbert: St Cuthbert arrives at Melrose (Oxford, University College Library MS 165, p. 23).*

was looked after by a foster mother by the name of Coenswith. Two miracles associated with his early life reveal that he spent some time as a shepherd, and that he also did some military service. He entered the monastery at Melrose when Boisil was prior, probably about 651 (**31**), but a few years later he moved to Eata's new foundation of Ripon, where he was employed as guestmaster. Probably as a consequence of the lobbying of Wilfrid of Hexham, the Northumbrian king soon evicted Eata and his community from their new found-

32 *St Cuthbert prays and teaches (Oxford, University College Library MS165, p.78)*

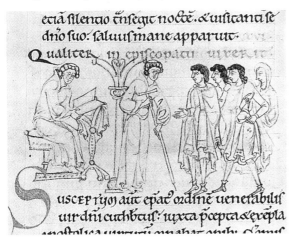

ation, which was handed over to Wilfrid. Eata and Cuthbert returned to Melrose for a time; Cuthbert appears to have joined the Lindisfarne community as prior some time after the Synod of Whitby, when Eata became Abbot of Lindisfarne in place of Colman.

In the course of his active career Cuthbert travelled all over northern England, and into Pictland, although he does not appear to have been as closely involved with secular authorities as some of his contemporaries. Towards the end of his career he seems to have adopted an increasingly ascetic and solitary lifestyle, retreating initially to his private cell on St Cuthbert's Island, and later to Inner Farne. He was persuaded to return to a more active pastoral role as Bishop of Lindisfarne for the last two years of his life (**32**), but died in his hermitage on Farne on 20 March, 687, attended by a small group of brethren. On his death, and more or less against his own wishes, his body was transported back to Lindisfarne. It was the discovery of his miraculously preserved corpse eleven years later, however, which guaranteed that his deeds and works would become widely known (**33**). His posthumous pre-eminence guaranteed that of his community also, and may be seen as responsible, either directly or indirectly, for the production of the masterpieces of early medieval art associated with the Anglo-Saxon monastery in the eighth and ninth centuries.

The Lindisfarne Gospels
The most famous of these products is undoubtedly the manuscript known popularly as the Lindisfarne Gospels, and professionally as B.M. (British Museum) Cotton Nero D IV. It is one of the best preserved and elaborate of a group of early medieval insular gospel books, and is of particular importance to art historians because both its place and date of production are known. It remained in the possession of the Community of St Cuthbert throughout the Middle Ages, though it is not clear whether it was kept at Durham or Lindisfarne. At the

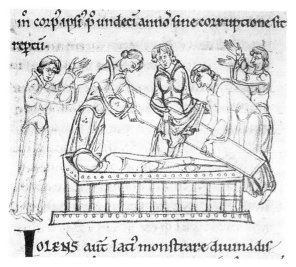

33 The monks find St Cuthbert's body still incorrupt
(Oxford, University College Library MS 165, p. 118).

Dissolution, it presumably fell into the hands of Henry VIII's commissioners: in the later part of the sixteenth century it belonged to Robert Bowyer, the Keeper of Records at the Tower of London. From him it passed in turn to Sir Robert Cotton, a great collector of old manuscripts, whose library formed one of the core collections of the British Museum when this was founded in 1752.

The gospels may have been prepared as a special treasure for the shrine of the saint when the cult of Cuthbert was initiated. In the later tenth century, when the book was at Chester-le-Street, a monk by the name of Aldred translated its contents into Old English in between the lines of the original text. A short note (known as a colophon) was added at this time, stating that Aldred himself, Eadfrith, Aethelwold and Bilfrith the anchorite were responsible for the production of the book. Eadfrith is credited with the writing and illumination of the text, Aethelwold with manufacture of an ornamental binding, and Bilfrith with its adornment with precious metals and gems. The last name is otherwise unknown, but Eadfrith and Aethelwold were both bishops of Lindisfarne, in 698–721 and 721–*c.*740 respectively. Although the colophon is a later

addition its ascription is generally accepted; and this means that we can be reasonably confident that the Lindisfarne Gospels were written in the late seventh or early part of the eighth century. It has been estimated that it would have taken the artist/scribe at least two years of full-time labour to produce such a complex manuscript. It is therefore all the more remarkable that the manuscript was the product of a single hand, who prepared both the text and the illuminations. Some scholars have speculated that it is unlikely that Eadfrith would have had the time to work on such a mammoth task while he was actually bishop, and date the book to the period when he was still an ordinary member of the community, before 698. Alternatively, he may have set about his task as a direct response to the discovery of the miraculous preservation of Cuthbert's body.

The version of the gospel text in the Book of

34 The Lindisfarne Gospels: canon tables
(British Library, Cotton Nero D IV, f. 11).

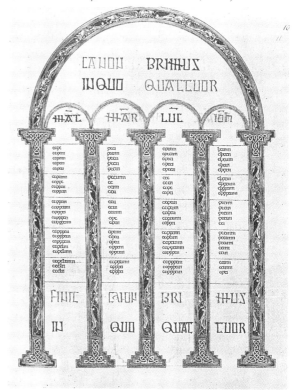

Lindisfarne is that known as the Vulgate, which was prepared by St Jerome in the later fourth century, and as well as the text of the gospels themselves there is additional material, which acts as a preface and introduction. At the very beginning of the book is a letter from Jerome to Pope Damasus, and a prologue to St Jerome's commentary on the gospel of Matthew. This is followed by a series of tables which show correspondence and concordance between the different gospels. These are known as Eusebian Canon Tables after the fourth-century theologian Eusebius who devised them. Each gospel is also preceded by a brief introduction or *argumentum*, and lists of liturgical readings and festivals. Scholars believe that the text of the gospel was copied from an Italian original, which was presumably a possession of the Lindisfarne monastery at the end of the seventh century.

The decoration of the manuscript conforms to a pattern found in other books of the period. At the beginning of the book, the letter from St Jerome to Pope Damasus is treated as a full-page initial. The canon tables (**34**) are divided by columns and linked by arcades filled with abstract and animal ornament. Each gospel is then preceded by a full-page illustration of the appropriate evangelist, accompanied by his symbol: for Matthew, a man (**35**); for Mark, a lion; for Luke, a calf; and for John, an eagle. This is followed by a page of elaborate ornament structured around a cross, and known as a cross-carpet page (**colour plate 6**); a similar page is also found before the letter to Pope Damasus. The first words of each gospel then follow, also elaborately decorated (**colour plate 7**). Other parts of the gospel deemed to be of particular importance are highlighted with decorated initials: the part of Matthew's gospel which gives the story of the birth of Christ is treated as a full-page illumination and there are many minor initials throughout the text. In all there are fifteen fully illuminated pages, as well as sixteen decorated pages of canon tables.

The decoration of the Lindisfarne Gospels owes much to contemporary styles of ornament, which have themselves very diverse origins. The elaborate spiral decoration (**36**a), for example, can be traced back to the art of the Celtic Iron Age, while the zoomorphic or animal-headed interlace (**36**b) is derived from Germanic metalwork. There is a particular emphasis on bird decoration in the manuscript (**36**c), and many have sought the inspiration for this in the rich bird-life of the island itself: particularly the cormorants and shags whose long necks and gleaming plumage find substantial echo in the sinuous lines and carefully depicted feathers of the birds in the manuscript. This interpretation is not wholly acceptable to scholars, who point out that the manuscript birds are hardly naturalistic representations of these species; for instance, they have long talons and claws which are drawn from late antique models. The imagery of birds is also a conspicuous feature

35 *The Lindisfarne Gospels: symbol of St Matthew* (British Library, Cotton Nero D IV, f. 25ᵛ).

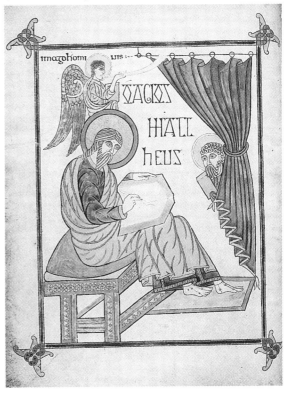

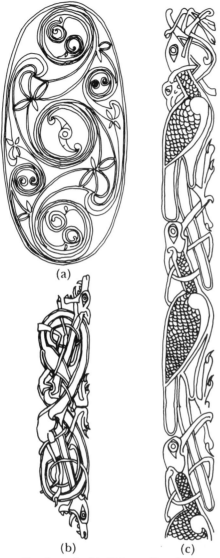

(a)

(b)   (c)

36 *Decoration from the Lindisfarne Gospels.*

local, others more exotic, such as the blue lapis lazuli, which may have come from Asia. The manuscript was made from calfskin vellum, and it has been estimated that at least 129 separate skins were required to produce the 258 individual leaves.

Although the decorative repertoire of the manuscript is shared by other forms of contemporary Northumbrian art, the portraits of the evangelists are totally unlike the normal representations of this subject in other insular manuscripts, and it is clear that Eadfrith was inspired by a very different model from that usually used by insular illuminators. There is an excellent clue to his source in the portrait of St Matthew. A manuscript produced at the monastery of Jarrow, a copy of an Italian bible known as the *Codex Amiatinus*, has a full-page picture of the scribe Ezra which closely

37 *The portrait of Ezra the scribe from the* Codex Amiatinus *(Biblioteca Medicea-Laurenziana, Florence, Amiatinus I, f. V)*

of the poem *de Abbatibus*. Even if the birds are not drawn from nature, however, their very abundance suggests that they may still have been inspired by it.

Whilst the designs appear spontaneous and free-flowing, the patterns have been carefully constructed using an elaborate framework of grids and compass-drawn circles – carefully though faintly pricked out on the manuscript page. The pigments used to provide the palate of brown, red, green, yellow, blue, pink and purple came from many different sources, some

38 *The Durham Gospels: the Crucifixion*
*(*Durham Cathedral Library A II 17, f. 38 3ᵛ).

resembles the Matthew portrait (**37**), and it seems certain that the two pictures share a common model, presumably an Italian gospel or bible, perhaps the very source of the gospel text copied by the Lindisfarne scribe.

Other Lindisfarne manuscripts

A number of other decorated manuscripts of the early Middle Ages are closely linked to the Lindisfarne Gospels. The best known of these are two other illuminated gospel books, the Durham Gospels, (known officially as Durham Cathedral Library A II 17) now displayed in the Treasury at Durham Cathedral, and the Echternach Gospels (Paris Bibl. Nat. MS lat. 9389) which were taken from their original

home at the monastery of Echternach in Switzerland to Paris in the eighteenth century. Fragments of a fourth gospel book, now split between two manuscripts (B.M. Cotton Otho C V and Corpus Christi College, Cambridge MS 197 B) are usually also seen as a part of the group. It is probable that these manuscripts were products of the monastic scriptorium on Lindisfarne, although scholars are not uniformly agreed on this point.

The Durham Gospels must once have been a splendid manuscript similar to the Lindisfarne Gospels, but unfortunately only a small part of its decorated pages remain. It may have contained a similar arrangement of evangelist portraits and cross-carpet pages at the beginning of each gospel but only a single full-page miniature painting of the Crucifixion survives (**38**), at the end of St Matthew's Gospel. Of

39 *The Durham Gospels: decorated initial at the beginning of St John's Gospel* (Durham Cathedral Library A II 17, f. 2).

40 *The Echternach Gospels: quarter-page initial (Bibliothèque Nationale LAT 9389 f. 19).*

the decorated initial pages only that at the beginning of St John's Gospel is still extant (**39**), but there are some major and many smaller decorated initials throughout the text. Later additions to the manuscript show that, like the Lindisfarne Gospels, the manuscript was with the Cuthbert community at Chester-le-Street in the tenth century. Also, there are corrections on it in the same handwriting as that used to correct the liturgical additions to the Lindisfarne Gospels.

The Echternach Gospels is a well-preserved manuscript, but the decoration is much simpler and also more limited: fewer colours are used, there are no carpet pages and the beginnings of the gospel are introduced by quarter- rather than full-page initials (**40**). There are full-page representations of the evangelist symbols (**colour plate 8**), but the use of interlace and abstract ornament is limited, and there is no animal ornament, although there are again many individually illuminated initials within

the text. Three of the frames of the evangelist-symbol pages are blank, suggesting that the manuscript is unfinished. The depiction of the St Matthew symbol is complete and of some interest, however, as it shows a man with a carefully drawn Roman tonsure. The monastery at Echternach was founded by the Northumbrian St Willebrord in 697/8, about the same time as the translation of the relics of St Cuthbert. Echternach was not founded as a daughter house of Lindisfarne but it has been suggested that the gospel book might have been a foundation-gift from the Lindisfarne community. Complex and elaborate animal ornament may have been deliberately avoided because the manuscript was required for a 'deadline'.

The fragmented and badly damaged Otho/Corpus Gospels contain two full-page evangelist symbols fairly close to those in the Echternach Gospels (**41**); surviving fragments indicate that it was originally decorated in a more lavish style. Little is known of its history before modern times, but there is some indirect evidence that at least that part of it now at Cambridge was at Canterbury in the sixteenth century.

Particularly close links have been identified between the Durham and Echternach Gospels. Study of the details of calligraphy and drawing in the two manuscripts has led to the conclusion

41 *The Otho/Corpus Gospels: symbol of St Mark (British Library, Cotton Otho C V f. 27).*

42 *Insular half-uncial script: Otho Gospels*
(British Library Cotton Otho C V f. 25ᵛ).

In spite of a common place of origin, however, there are considerable differences between the manuscripts in terms of versions of the gospel text, iconography, style of ornament and arrangement of the leaves or folios. Even the arrangement of the lines of text varies: in the Durham and Otho/Corpus Gospels it runs continuously across and down the page, but in Lindisfarne and Echternach it is arranged in two parallel columns, and broken up into individual clauses (*per cola et commata*). There was clearly little absolute standardization.

Scholarly attention has naturally focused on the elaborately ornamented gospel books, but it should be remembered that they probably represent only a tiny proportion of the output of the Lindisfarne scriptorium. The everyday work of the monastic scribes would have consisted of a fairly wide range of unilluminated texts – psalters, commentaries, saints' lives etc., intended for study and everyday devotion. Surviving examples of these works can occasionally be recognized as Lindisfarne products because they make use of the distinctive Lindisfarne script.

The very complexity of the relationships between text, script, ornament and format in the great gospel books offers some insight into the cultural and ecclesiastical contacts of the island monastery. The early medieval manuscripts preserved at Durham since the Middle Ages, the majority of which would surely have been acquired while the community was still on Lindisfarne, include a number of books from the scriptorium of Wearmouth/Jarrow. This suggests that there was substantial local exchange of manuscripts, although it is conceivable that these were acquired as a 'job-lot' when Wearmouth and Jarrow were abandoned. We can only speculate about the precise contents of the monastic library in the Golden Age, but in addition to the works produced in the monastery itself, it would have contained many other works which had been received as gifts, exchanged or acquired abroad; in turn, books made on Lindisfarne would have been

that they are both products of the same hand, the Echternach Gospels probably broadly contemporary with the Lindisfarne Gospels, the Durham Gospels slightly later. The Otho/Corpus Gospels are, similarly, usually dated to the early eighth century.

In all the manuscripts, the script generally used for the main gospel text has heavy round letters, which are closely confined within the space allotted to the line. This is a distinctive form of the script known as Insular half-uncial or Insular majescule (**42, 43**). Many scholars are of the opinion that this style of writing was developed on Lindisfarne in the eighth century. Likewise, three of them – Lindisfarne, Durham and Echternach – are the products of a single artist/calligrapher, and this may have been a distinctive pattern of work in the Lindisfarne scriptorium.

43 *Insular half-uncial script: The Durham Gospels (Durham Cathedral Library A II 17 f.).*

dispatched to other houses of the Lindisfarne community, and other ecclesiastical foundations in both Britain and Europe.

In selecting gospel texts to copy, and illuminations to emulate, the Lindisfarne scribes would have had a range of different examples to serve as prototypes. It is usual to see insular manuscript art as highly traditional – stylistic innovation was not a goal in itself. However, the artist/scribe could exercise some choice in terms of the particular tradition selected and was not obliged to follow the latest version or fashion. Earlier works were still available as models, so were the products of a range of other monastic scriptoria. These could be adapted, and innovation was occasionally permissible to serve a worthy end: scholars have speculated

that the distinctive Roman tonsure of the man symbol of St Matthew in the Echternach Gospels was an encoded statement of the importance of adhering to Roman orthodoxy, for example. The questions of provenance and affinity which have obsessed many scholars are intractable at least partly because the cultural milieu which produced them had such close contacts with other monastic centres. As even the history of the known Lindisfarne manuscripts shows, books could travel far and wide in the early Middle Ages.

The relics of St Cuthbert

Cuthbert's physical relics were the greatest treasure of the Lindisfarne monks, and when the community finally decided to leave the island they were carefully removed, travelling all over the north of England until they arrived eventually at their present home in Durham Cathedral. Although it would be difficult to get a clear impression of the medieval magnificence of the shrine itself from what now survives, the relics offer a fascinating insight into Cuthbert and his cult, and highlight the importance of the Lindisfarne community in the early Middle Ages. Information about the relics is provided partly by historical sources and partly by the surviving material now on display in the cathedral at Durham. The coffin of St Cuthbert was opened on a number of occasions in medieval and modern times (see table p. **66**) and different accounts of these openings have survived.

In 698, the outer garments in which Cuthbert had been buried eleven years previously were removed, including his shoes, and these seem to have been accessible to visitors to the shrine in the early eighth century. His inner shroud or wrapping, which seems to have covered the whole of his body, was left in place. A new garment was put on the body which was then placed in a light chest on the floor of the sanctuary on Lindisfarne.

St Cuthbert's relics were placed inside the still unfinished Norman cathedral at Durham with great pomp and celebration in 1104. As part of the ceremonies surrounding the new translation, the coffin reliquary was publicly opened, to demonstrate the continuing miracle of preservation. Two detailed twelfth-century descriptions of this opening are known, one by an anonymous monk, the other by Reginald of Durham, a notable medieval historian and hagiographer who was also a member of the Durham community. Neither are contemporary with the events which they describe, but they clearly rely on authentic and quite detailed local information.

Inside the outer coffin the monks found a hide-covered, iron-bound chest, which contained the 'light chest' of 698, wrapped in a linen cloth. The lid was then lifted, and a copy of the gospels discovered, on a shelf by the head. When the shelf had been dismantled the body of Cuthbert was revealed, lying on its side. The coffin also held the relics of the other saints and bishops, which had been removed from Lindisfarne in 875. The monks removed the body from the coffin, and carefully examined the vestments and cloths in which it was wrapped, which are described by Reginald in great detail. A number of objects were found by the body: the accounts mention an ivory comb and a pair of scissors, a silver altar, a linen cloth 'for covering the sacramental elements', a paten and a chalice, 'small in size but from its materials and workmanship precious'. These were replaced when the body was returned to its coffin, but the other relics were kept, apart from the head of King Oswald.

The description of the shrine at the time of its destruction in 1538 is to be found in a work known as the *Rites of Durham*. The despoilers of the shrine broke open an outer, iron-bound chest, and within found Cuthbert

> ...whole, uncorrupt, with his face bare, and his beard as it had been a fortnight's growth, and all his vestments upon him as he was accustomed to say mass withall: and his metwand of gold lying beside him...

In their efforts to remove the body from the coffin one of the saint's legs was broken; it was then kept for a time in the vestry and ultimately reburied in 1542 on the site of the former shrine.

The accounts vary in detail, but on all of these occasions his flesh was apparently still preserved, reinforcing belief in the miraculous power of the saint. Modern scholars and theologians, more sceptical of miracles than their medieval predecessors, have occasionally doubted the veracity of contemporary accounts. However, this preservation was possibly a natural phenomenon: a number of accidentally-preserved medieval bodies are known, and it is possible that if Cuthbert had been buried in a well-sealed environment the processes of decay would not have advanced very far.

Only a skeleton remained, however, when

44 *The coffin of St Cuthbert (*Durham Cathedral Library*).*

the grave was reopened in 1827 by James Raine, Librarian of the Cathedral and the first modern Cuthbert scholar. In addition to the bones of the saint a number of objects were found inside a series of rather decayed oak coffins. Raine provided the first detailed discussion of the objects associated with the saint's body, and removed some of these from the tomb.

In 1899, the tomb was opened for the last time. The remaining fragments of textiles and coffins were not replaced on this occasion. The scholarly study of the relics took many decades but after careful conservation they have now been put on display in a special treasury at Durham Cathedral.

The skeleton of the saint was examined in 1899 before it was replaced. It was more or less complete (the left tibia was missing) and indicated that Cuthbert had been a man of medium height, about 172cm (5ft 8in) or 175cm (5ft 9in) tall, of muscular build, and probably in his late fifties when he died. There was some indication that he might have suffered from tuberculosis.

Some of the objects, and one of the coffins, date from the time of the original translation on Lindisfarne in 698. A number of items were probably added at later reopenings, and some of the objects described in the accounts discussed above, such as the chalice and paten of 1104, and the 'metwand' – possibly a crozier or staff – mentioned in 1538, do not now survive. Modern scholars have done their best to sort out this material, but doubt about the date of some items still lingers.

The series of up to four coffins seems to represent medieval attempts to preserve and conserve the original relics: at each opening, a stout new oak box was provided to hold the by now partly decayed predecessor. The innermost coffin (**44**) is generally recognized as the one into which the saint's body was moved in 698. It has been restored from many fragments, most recently in 1978. It was made originally from six separate planks of oak, all of which seem to have been cut from the same tree. All of the panels were decorated.

The coffin lid depicts Christ in majesty, surrounded by the symbols of the four evangelists. One of the ends of the coffin has a representation of the Virgin and Child. Images of the twelve Apostles, arranged in two tiers, are found on one of the long sides, and the other two

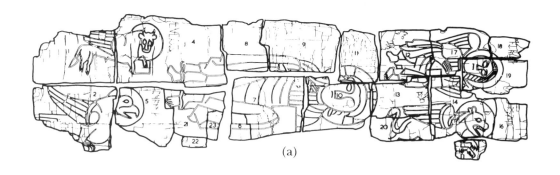

(a)

(b)

(c)

45 *The coffin of St Cuthbert: (a) Coffin lid: Christ in Majesty, surrounded by the symbols of the four evangelists; (b) the end panels: the Virgin and Child, and two Apostles; (c) the coffin sides: archangels and Apostles (after S. Dickinson).*

sides have representations of archangels. These figures are identified by short inscriptions in runic and Latin characters, although not all have survived (**45a,b,c**). The base panel was incised with a large cross with a stepped base, possibly a representation of a free-standing cross.

The Apostles are all depicted holding books, and are shown with long hair and without a beard. The exception is St Paul, who is shown with a beard; St Peter is likewise individually recognizable as he holds the keys to the Kingdom of Heaven. He has a clearly defined Roman tonsure, and it has been suggested that this was another 'visual slogan' of the Romanizing party in Northumberland, as in the depiction of the St Matthew symbol in the Echternach Gospels. Scholars are generally agreed that the representations of saints and angels are copied from Mediterranean models, which must have been available in some form in the monastery on Lindisfarne.

One of the small objects which may have belonged to St Cuthbert himself is a pectoral cross, a small gold ornament inlaid with cut garnets which may have represented some kind of badge of office or official gift (**colour plate 9**). It was not noted in 1104 or 1538, and first discovered at the 1827 opening of the tomb in a rather fragmentary condition, close to the body of the saint among the inner wrappings.

In the early part of the seventh century, Anglo-Saxon jewellers of eastern and southern England were producing magnificent jewellery of this type, best exemplified by the treasures of Sutton Hoo. However, this style of jewellery seems to have gone out of fashion by the end of the century, and there is not much evidence for its popularity in Northumbria, although this may be partly due to the erratic nature of archaeological survival. The cross differs in some details of its manufacture from other English jewellery of this type; however, current scholarly consensus recognizes it as probably a northern product. It shows signs of multiple repair, suggesting that it was hardly new when it was buried.

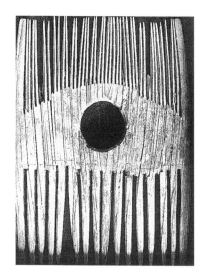

46 *The comb from St Cuthbert's coffin* (Durham Cathedral Library).

A double-sided comb, clearly that described in detail in 1104, was discovered by Raine 'among the uppermost garments of the saint, upon the lower part of the breast'. The comb is made from a single slab of African ivory and as now restored it is quite large (11.83cm × 16.3cm (4 ½in × 6½in); (**46**). There is a large central perforation and the teeth on one side are fine, on the other coarse.

Reginald of Durham recounts how the sacristan Aelfred Westou, who had the care of Cuthbert's relics in the middle of the eleventh century, used to dress the still growing hair of the saint, with a comb and a pair of silver scissors, which he had made especially for the purpose. Raine assumed that the comb found by him was made by Aelfred Westou, and it is certainly totally unlike the normal types of Anglo-Saxon bone comb, but also difficult to place in an eleventh-century milieu. In 1956 it was identified as a genuine relic of the time of Cuthbert, though clearly of exotic, and probably Coptic, origin.

A rectangular wooden tablet covered with silver, and now known as St Cuthbert's portable altar, was also noted in 1104 and removed from the tomb in 1827. The oak tablet itself is simply decorated with five incised crosses, one in the centre and one in each of the four corners. There is also an inscription running across the

47 *St Cuthbert's wooden altar (Durham Cathedral Library).*

lower part of this upper face, which reads '+ in honour of St Peter' (**47**). At a later stage the altar was enshrined in a silver cover, decorated with ornamental foliage and a human figure (**48**). Too little of this cover now survives to identify this figure with certainty, but St Peter has been proposed as a likely candidate. The original wood may have been left exposed in a central space, but this was later covered by an ornamental roundel.

The wooden tablet may well have been the property of the saint himself but the date of its silver 'shrine' is less certain. The decoration of the shrine is stylistically unlikely to be as early as the seventh or as late as the twelfth century, but the cover may have been made either when the community was still on Lindisfarne, or during their stay at Chester-le-Street. The fact that the central area of the altar was left exposed suggests that it was probably accessible for worshippers at the shrine to touch, rather than concealed in the closed coffin, and this is borne out by one of the accounts of the 1104

48 *The silver covering of St Cuthbert's altar (Durham Cathedral Library).*

opening, which implies that it was on a shelf above the body.

The small copy of St John's Gospels, now on display in the British Library but the property of Stonyhurst College and therefore known as either the Cuthbert or Stonyhurst Gospels, was removed from the coffin in 1104, and carries a twelfth-century inscription to that effect. It is the only surviving example of an early medieval manuscript in its original decorated binding from the whole of western Europe. The text is without decoration, but on the basis of the script and the version of the gospel text used in the manuscript, it is recognized as a product of the scriptorium of Wearmouth/Jarrow. St Cuthbert is thought to have had a particular

1 *St Cuthbert's Island at sunset.*

2 *Lindisfarne from the air* (© Aerofilms).

3 *Digital Terrain Model of the medieval land surface around Green Shiel.*

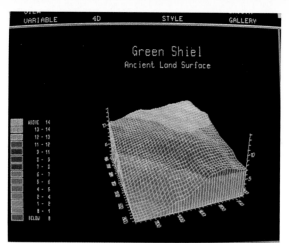

4 *Artist's impression of the Anglo-Saxon monastery on Lindisfarne (drawn by Peter Dunn; English Heritage).*

5 *Reconstruction of St Cuthbert's cell on Farne (drawn by Peter Dunn; English Heritage).*

6 *The Lindisfarne Gospels:
cross-carpet page* (British Library
Cotton Nero D IV, f. 138ᵛ).

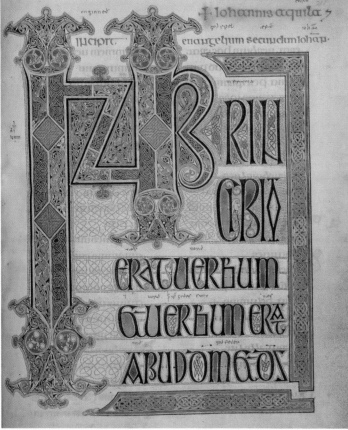

7 *The Lindisfarne Gospels:
full-page initial at the beginning of
St John's Gospel*
(British Library Cotton Nero
D IV, f. 211).

8 *The Echternach Gospels: symbol of St Matthew* (Bibliothèque Nationale, Paris LAT 9389, f. 18ᵛ).

9 *St Cuthbert's pectoral cross* (Durham Cathedral Library).

10 *Green Shiel: Building C in the course of excavation.*

11 *Green Shiel: the east end of Building B, showing partition wall and paving slabs.*

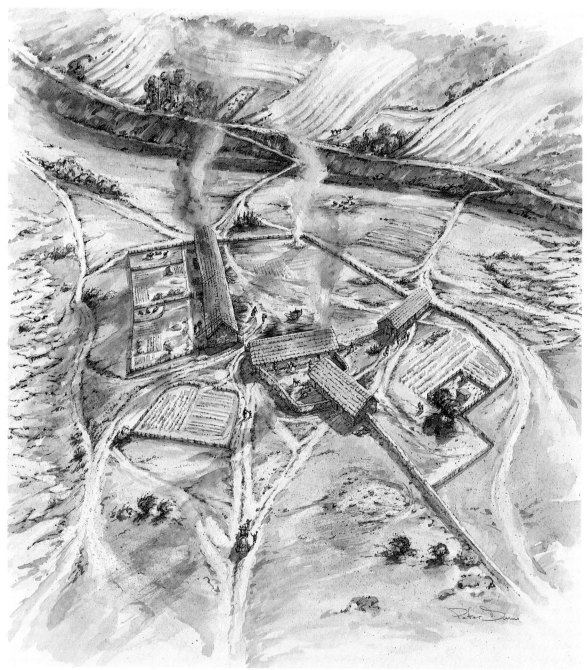

12 *Reconstruction drawing of the site at Green Shiel* (drawn by Peter Dunn; English Heritage).

13 *Reconstruction of the nave of the priory church* (drawn by Terry Ball; English Heritage).

14 *Post-medieval imported slipware dish found in the priory* (English Heritage).

devotion to St John's Gospel, and the placing of the book within the coffin reinforces this connection, although the book itself is usually dated to the end of the seventh or early eighth century, possibly a gift from the monks of Wearmouth/Jarrow to the new shrine of the saint.

The rich liturgical vestments described in 1104 have mostly only survived in small fragments, but they provide interesting evidence of the quality of offerings made to the shrine, and also of early openings of the coffin which are otherwise undocumented or poorly documented, when offerings must have been placed around the body.

It is known that Aethelstan visited the shrine at Chester-le-Street *c*.934, and a stole and two maniples, which are quite well preserved, are presumably those noted in the account of his gifts to the shrine. Both the stole and the larger of the two maniples have identical inscriptions which state that they were made by Queen Aelflaed for Bishop Frithestan (**49**). Aelflaed was Aethelstan's stepmother and died in 916; Frithestan was Bishop of Winchester from 909 to 931. The embroideries were therefore clearly made in southern England, a couple of decades before the presentation, and not necessarily with Cuthbert in mind. The skill of English embroidresses was famous throughout Europe at this time, but the vestments from the coffin are among the very few survivals of this art.

Among the other textile pieces are several which are also clearly later than the time of Cuthbert. Several miscellaneous fragments have been reconstructed as an Anglo-Saxon dalmatic, or tunic, of eighth- or ninth-century date, made from imported silks and braids. There are also many fragments of a Byzantine patterned wrapping, known as the Nature Goddess silk. This seems to have been made in the eighth or ninth century: it is possible that it was also given by Aethelstan, who included seven *pallia* or ceremonial wraps among his gifts. Alternatively, it may be one of the Greek *pallia* presented to the shrine by King Edmund

c. 945. The remains of two other patterned wrappings, known as the Rider and Peacock silks, are later in date and probably Spanish Islamic work of the tenth, eleventh or twelfth centuries. A thirteenth-century ring now in Ushaw College, Durham was allegedly found on the body of Cuthbert at the Reformation, although it is not mentioned in the *Rites of Durham*.

The cult of Cuthbert at Durham remained very important throughout the Middle Ages, and many new 'traditions' developed around him, the most famous of which was an extreme misogyny, not at all evidenced in the contemporary sources for his life. The cult only came to an end when the shrine housing his body was demolished on the orders of Henry VIII's commissioners at the Dissolution. The refoundation of the priory on Lindisfarne at the end of the eleventh century was largely an act of piety and veneration for Cuthbert's original resting-place, and the island was itself a place of pilgrimage, although the vital relics were kept elsewhere.

49 *Reverse end of the stole found in St Cuthbert's coffin, showing inscription:* AElfflaed fieri precepit (Durham Cathedral Library).

The movements and openings of St Cuthbert and his coffin

687: St Cuthbert dies on Farne, but is buried in the church on Lindisfarne.

698: The grave of Cuthbert is opened, and his body found to be incorrupt. It is moved to a new resting-place inside the church, and a major cult is initiated.

84?: St Cuthbert's relics are moved to Norham for safety for a period.

875: The shrine of Cuthbert on Lindisfarne is dismantled, and the community travel with it around northern England, eventually settling at Chester-le-Street in 883.

934: Aethelstan presents a number of offerings to the shrine of Cuthbert, and the coffin is opened so that some of these can be placed in direct association with the saint.

c. *944*: Kind Edmund visits the shrine and presents offerings.

995: The Cuthbert community abandons Chester-le-Street, taking the relics with them. They find a brief refuge at Ripon, moving from there to settle at Durham.

1069–70: St Cuthbert's shrine returns to Lindisfarne for protection for three months, during William the Conqueror's 'Harrying of the North'.

August, 1104: The translation of St Cuthbert's relics to a new shrine behind the high altar at Durham Cathedral takes place, in preparation for which his coffin is opened.

1538: The shrine of St Cuthbert is demolished by the commissioners of Henry VIII. The grave is opened, and the still uncorrupted body found.

1542: St Cuthbert is reburied on the site of his former shrine, behind the high altar at Durham.

1827: The grave of Cuthbert is opened by Raine. The body is now reduced to a skeleton.

1899: St Cuthbert's grave is opened for the last time, by Canon Greenwell.

1956: The contents of St Cuthbert's grave are definitively published.

1978: The fragments of the saint's coffin are conserved and remounted and a new display of the relics is opened in the undercroft of Durham Cathedral.

1987: In commemoration of the 1300th anniversary of his death, the Lindisfarne Gospels are returned briefly to the tomb of the saint.

6

The medieval priory

In 1083 the Community of St Cuthbert at Durham, that body of clerics which could demonstrate direct descent from the seventh-century monks of Lindisfarne, was presented with an ultimatum by the newly appointed Bishop of Durham, William of St Calais: to become monks in the Benedictine monastery he intended to serve his cathedral church, or to leave. All but two chose the latter alternative, and the treasures of the community, together with the lion's share of its extensive estates, were transferred to the incoming Benedictines. Given their origins in such dubious circumstances, it is hardly surprising that the earliest generations of Durham monks were preoccupied with convincing themselves and others of their claim to be considered the rightful guardians of St Cuthbert's shrine, and the legitimate heirs of the monks who had founded the monastery on Lindisfarne almost five hundred years before. It is only against this background that the close interest taken in the island by the monks in the early twelfth century can be properly understood.

The earliest evidence centres on the activities of a Durham monk called Edward, who had organized the building of a new church on Lindisfarne in honour of St Cuthbert in or before 1122. This was almost certainly intended to provide an appropriate setting for the original burial place of St Cuthbert, since a 'tomb of the blessed Cuthbert which is within the church' is mentioned later in the twelfth century. The grave had presumably been in the open since the timber church of St Peter in which it had originally been housed had been removed by the Anglo-Saxon monks when they left the island in the ninth century, but it is reasonable to suppose that such a sacred spot would have been known and revered throughout the intervening centuries. It has generally been assumed that the existing romanesque church can be identified with Edward's building. This cannot be regarded as certain, however, for the provision of comparatively small yet architecturally impressive stone churches at sites which were superseded by larger and more elaborate ones within a generation of their construction can be paralleled at other sites in the twelfth century, and only excavation might now reveal whether Edward's effort related to a structure preceding the present one. If that is the case, it must rapidly have been replaced, for the style of the extant ruins (**50**) indicates that this church must have been completed by *c.* 1150 at the latest.

The new church was small in size compared to other great romanesque churches of its day (its length was less than two-fifths that of its great counterpart at Durham itself, for example), but its architectural form was remarkably elaborate given its modest dimensions. Cruciform in plan, with an aisleless chancel and transepts, each with an apse opening to the east, and with an aisled nave of six bays (**51**), the dominant external feature would

50 *The priory ruins from the Heugh.*

have been a high tower at the crossing, probably capped originally by a low pyramidal spire. The three eastern limbs had two storeys, but in the nave a miniature version of the three-storeyed elevation characteristic of the great churches of Anglo-Norman England was adopted. The west front, with its prominent flanking stair turrets, also seems to have been intended to recall the imposing twin-towered west facades common in larger churches. The other notably prestigious feature of the design was the provision of stone vaults throughout. This was rare indeed in English architecture of the period, and was surely influenced by the decision to execute a similarly comprehensive scheme of vaulting at Durham Cathedral itself. Other features of the design of Lindisfarne, most notably the use of two pier designs,

those with compound shafts alternating with cylinders with incised geometrical decoration, are clearly derived from the design of Durham.

The provision of a church considerably more elaborate than its dimensions might have led one to expect, is presumably a consequence of the principal motif underlying its erection, that is, the desire of the Durham monks to provide a grand architectural setting for the site of the grave of their patron saint. What is more, the parallels with Durham may be significant in this respect. While it is possible that some merely reflect the practical considera-tion that the masons in the region most easily accessible to the Durham monks at the time were to be found among those building the cathedral, it seems likely that the choice of other features, such as the three-storeyed ele-vation of the nave, stone vaulting throughout and the treatment of the west front, were

51 *The nave of the priory church.*

deliberate attempts to recreate the architecture of the great cathedral church in miniature at Lindisfarne. It would thus have become a visual expression of the link between the original and final resting-places of Cuthbert's relics which the first Durham monks were so anxious to reinforce.

If the purposes of the Durham monks in building the new church at Lindisfarne are reasonably clear, the precise ways in which it initially functioned and was staffed are less so. One thing seems reasonably certain: the church cannot have been intended to have had any parochial functions, for these were almost certainly centred on the church of St Mary immediately to the west. Whatever the date of the early fabric in this latter building (see above, Chapter 4), there must certainly have been a stone church here by the late eleventh century, and the chances are that pastoral activity had been associated with St Mary's at least by the time that the new church was begun, and probably for a long time before. While the presence of Cuthbert's cenotaph in the new church might at first indicate that it was primarily designed to accommodate an extensive pilgrimage traffic, the evidence of the twelfth-century miracle stories associated with St Cuthbert suggests that it was the site of his hermitage on Farne Island, rather than that of his burial place on Lindisfarne near by, which was the contemporary focus of popular devotion. This disparity only serves to strengthen the suggestion that the erection of the new church was primarily of significance for the Durham monastic community itself. The obvious inference would therefore be that it was intended from the beginning (as it certainly became from the later twelfth century) to be the church of a priory dependent on Durham itself and staffed by Durham monks. Yet this is not as easily demonstrable as might be supposed, for the earliest clear documentary reference to a monastic community dates only from the early 1170s, a generation after the church was completed; while the arrangement of its doorways on the south side seems difficult to reconcile with the provision of monastic buildings on the conventional claustral arrangement. On the other hand, the design of the church seems to have provided for at least three altars (one in each apse) from the beginning, which surely indicates that it was intended to be staffed by a community of some kind; and given the significance of the site to the Durham monks, it seems inconceivable that they could have contemplated anyone other than from among their own number. Perhaps, then, the first monks were too few to have warranted the erection of claustral buildings of the classic monastic type, and lived instead in simple (and perhaps at this date, timber) domestic buildings, probably to the south of the church, which were only replaced later as numbers increased. If so, the concentration of early building activity on the church and not, as was the regular practice elsewhere, on the monks' quarters, must again be seen as a consequence of the wholly exceptional significance of the site to the priory at Durham.

Two features may indicate that the number of monks in the newly established community grew rapidly during the middle and late twelfth century. First, the principal apse of the new church was demolished and the chancel doubled in length and given a square east end in a late romanesque style, which seems unlikely to date from much later than *c.* 1160. While it is always possible that this reflects changes in liturgical practice now irrecoverable, it may simply reflect an increased demand for space to house more monks in the choir. Second, the style of the west range of the monastic buildings suggest that it may date from as early as the late twelfth century; by this time, therefore, the size (and resources) of the community apparently warranted the beginning of a claustral complex, which suggests that a fully fledged community of a prior and twelve monks was at least anticipated, though it remains uncertain whether such numbers were ever actually reached. To judge from the scant surviving remains, the other two ranges of the cloister were completed in the earlier thirteenth century. The eastern one contained, as usual, a chapter house on the ground floor with the dormitory above it, while the south range housed the refectory, with kitchen and other domestic offices to the west separated by a screens passage.

The new priory of Lindisfarne was only one of a number of monasteries dependent on the cathedral-priory of Durham, most of which had come into existence by the late twelfth century. They ranged in size from Coldingham, a few miles north of Lindisfarne in Berwickshire, which accommodated as many as thirty monks at its peak in the thirteenth century, to small cells like Farne, which rarely accommodated more than two monks. The development of the buildings at Lindisfarne suggests that it lay between these two extremes. The majority of the cells were kept most of the time firmly under the control of the mother-house. What did this mean in practice? First, unlike an independent monastery at which monks made their professions to their superior, all the monks who staffed the cells were professed at Durham, and would thus have thought of themselves as monks of the mother-house. Second, they were sent out from Durham to serve at a cell, moved from one cell to another, or back to Durham itself, as the Prior of Durham thought fit.

These two features effectively counteracted any tendency for the cells to build up any degree of self-identity as communities, or for their heads to be tempted to wrest a degree of independence from the mother-house (a temptation to which the Prior of Coldingham succumbed unsuccessfully in the thirteenth century). Durham maintained an equally tight control over the cells' financial affairs, each superior being obliged to draw up an annual account of his receipts and expenditure and whenever possible to travel to Durham in person once a year to present this for audit at the convent's annual general chapter. Besides this supervisory role, Durham had the power to impose levies on its cells to assist the purposes of the mother-house. This power was exercised increasingly frequently in the more difficult financial climate of the later Middle Ages, and had become a regular annual charge from the mid-fifteenth century, which must have been a considerable drain on the cells' (by then already much depleted) resources. In contrast, the cells were expected to be financially independent of the mother-house, so could not expect much help in periods of difficulty.

Besides being a distinctive feature of life in the Durham monastic community, providing the monks with more variation in routine than was usually available elsewhere, the cells were one of the ways in which Durham reinforced its pre-eminence in the religious life of the north-east. Five of them (Lindisfarne and Farne Island in Northumberland, and Finchale, Jarrow and Wearmouth in Co. Durham) were located in the region, giving the Durham community a significant presence there. What is more, Durham's dominant position was jealously guarded, discouraging rival foundations. Thus Tynemouth was the only Benedictine monastery in the area not under Durham's control, while in the northern half of Northumberland, only the Premonstratensian canons of Alnwick offered any serious competition to the Durham monks on Lindisfarne.

The cell on Lindisfarne derived its income from two sources: property and tithes. Of the first, by far the most important was the manor of Fenham, on the mainland opposite the south-west corner of the island. Until it was leased for a cash rent in the early fifteenth century, this served as a kind of home farm for the priory, supplying much of the produce it consumed. Here also was a corn mill, from which the monks derived a steady source of income. But by far the most important element in the priory's resources, at least until the early fourteenth century, was its right to the corn-tithes of the parish of Lindisfarne. The medieval parish, whose extent probably fossilized to a considerable degree the original landed endowment of the Anglo-Saxon monastery, took in a substantial area of the adjacent mainland as well as of the island itself. In the later twelfth and thirteenth centuries, when population levels seem to have been increasing and the amount of cultivated land with them, this represented a very considerable asset which the monks might choose either to consume in kind or sell for cash. But its value was only as great as the land being tithed, and circumstances conspired to diminish it drastically in the course of the first half of the fourteenth century.

The first factor behind this was the destabilization of the area, lying as it did immediately adjacent to the Scottish border, following the outbreak of war with Scotland in 1296. At first it seemed that these disruptions might have been of a temporary and reversible nature, but as the fourteenth century wore on it became apparent that among the repercussions of the conflict were permanent social and economic decline. These difficulties were considerably exacerbated by the impact of the Black Death in 1348 and the subsequent outbreaks of plague. The depopulation consequent upon these upheavals reduced demand for corn and left far fewer people on the land who were able to produce it. The income from tithes therefore plummeted, and though there were periods of partial recovery, it was never to return to levels remotely approaching what had been attained

71

THE SOUTH VIEW OF HOLY ISLAND MONASTERY & CASTLE BELONGING TO THE BISHOPRICK OF DURHAM

52 *Engraving of the priory c. 1720, by S. Buck.*

before the early fourteenth century. In 1327 a monastic accountant bewailed the fact that the tithes which had been worth £107 'before the war' were now worth a mere £21.

The implications of this change in circumstances must have been immediate and dramatic. The priory's income was no longer sufficient to sustain the number of monks which had been supported in the thirteenth century – it had been reduced to five by the fourteenth century and to a mere three by the fifteenth. The monastic buildings thus needed to be adapted in two major respects: they had to be tailored to the needs of a much smaller community; and they had to be able to protect that community from external attack. The date at which the fortification of the priory was carried out is not known precisely, though such scant architectural detail as there is suggests a date in the earlier fourteenth century. The church itself was included in the defences, being provided with low-pitched roofs with battlemented parapets and (in the upper part of the west gable at least) arrow-slits. The

perimeter wall, with its wall-walk, enclosed the guesthouse and all the service buildings of the outer court as well as the living quarters of the monks, and this may have meant some contraction in the extent of the buildings compared to the thirteenth-century ones. The porch to the refectory, which also controlled access to the claustral buildings, was given additional outer defences, effectively dividing up the buildings like the outer and inner wards of a castle. The prior's lodging, at the south-east corner of the claustral buildings, was given particularly strong defences. This may be due to the fact that, like its counterpart at the cell at Finchale, the prior's lodging became the focus of the life of the reduced community, which became organized less formally than before on lines resembling those of a domestic household. The addition of a bakehouse and brewhouse immediately west of the kitchen presumably replaced earlier and perhaps more remotely situated ones which could not easily have been incorporated within the new walls.

It is worth noting that, despite the general picture of gloom which a description of the fourteenth-century developments tends to produce, the adaptation of the buildings and their equipment with new defences involved a considerable amount of expenditure, indicating that the priory, though it found itself in comparatively lean times, was by no means yet destitute. What is more, some of the alterations to the church in this period, involving the insertion of up-to-date traceried windows and the repainting of images, were decidedly non-utilitarian in character. Likewise, the provision of large late-medieval fireplaces and chimneys in the prior's lodging indicates that the monks might still expect a reasonable degree of personal comfort. It seems that the provision of strong defences proved a not entirely unmixed blessing, for in 1385 the priory petitioned the crown for permission to have them taken down. This may suggest that they made the priory the focus of conflict as often as they afforded protection from it; in any event, the evidence of the surviving ruins suggests that the petition proved unsuccessful. The occurrence in later inventories of stores of armour, weapons and gunpowder demonstrates that the need for defence was real enough.

The testimony of monks who were called upon to staff the priory at Lindisfarne about life there survives only from this period of uncertain times and depleted numbers in the later Middle Ages. The atmosphere of the priory must have changed out of all recognition from the thirteenth century, and this evidence cannot therefore be used to determine what life was like when numbers of monks and prosperity were at their height. To judge from the fact that most spells of service at Lindisfarne, as at the other Durham cells, were short, it was not regarded as a popular task by most of the monks, a suspicion confirmed by a letter from one of the fourteenth-century occupants of the cell to the Prior of Durham requesting permission to return to the mother-house. Equally, it would not usually have been in the Prior of Durham's interest to allow his monks to languish unhappily in this remote outpost of his empire, for monastic discipline could rapidly become slack in such circumstances; letters from the Prior of Durham admonishing his monks at Lindisfarne for (admittedly minor) lapses underline this point. It was thus in the interests of all parties to move the monks around comparatively frequently, exceptions being made only occasionally, perhaps for monks who had a genuine liking for the place or who may have had relations in the area and who wished to be near them in their old age.

The comparative security of the priory buildings meant that they offered refuge to others besides the Lindisfarne monks themselves. Thus their fellows from Farne Island were occasionally forced to abandon the cell there and move in; similarly, before its abandonment to the Scots in the 1460s, the monks of the Prior of Durham's northernmost cell of Coldingham might have found themselves at Lindisfarne when the political situation meant that they were unable to cross the border and occupy their own cell. The uncertain political situation seems to have induced some of the

53 *Nineteenth-century engraving of the priory* (*English Heritage*).

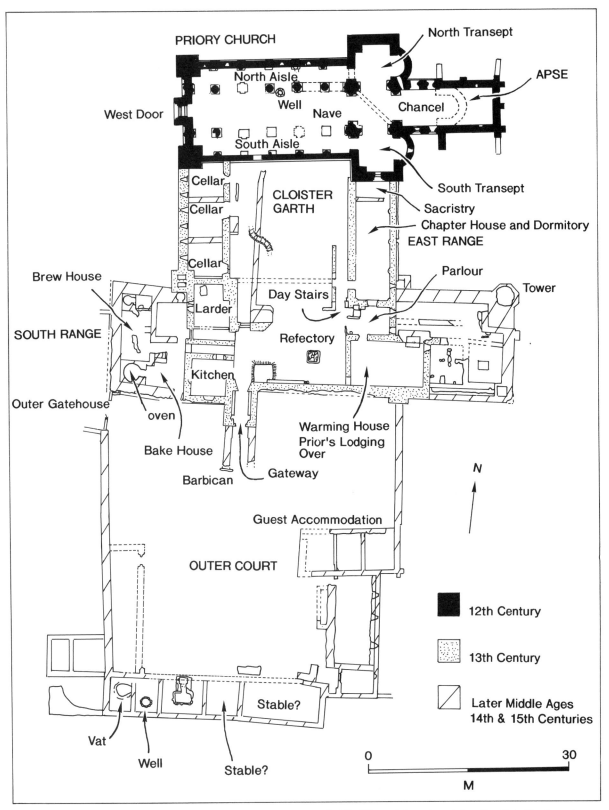

PRIORY CHURCH

North Transept

APSE

North Aisle

Well

Nave

Chancel

West Door

South Aisle

South Transept

Sacristy

Chapter House and Dormitory

EAST RANGE

Cellar

Cellar

CLOISTER GARTH

Cellar

Brew House

Parlour

Tower

Day Stairs

Larder

SOUTH RANGE

Refectory

Outer Gatehouse

Kitchen

oven

Bake House

Warming House
Prior's Lodging
Over

Barbican

Gateway

N

Guest Accommodation

OUTER COURT

12th Century

13th Century

Later Middle Ages
14th & 15th Centuries

0   30

M

Vat

Well

Stable?

Stable?

54 *The west door of the priory* (English Heritage).   ▲ 55 *Plan of the priory* (after English Heritage).

local parish clergy to lodge within the priory too as paying guests, perhaps supplying a much needed source of extra income for the monks.

Like Durham's other cells south of Tweed, the small community of monks at Lindisfarne endured the Dissolution of the lesser monasteries in 1536, when they were all vacated and the monks returned for the last time to the mother-house at Durham, thus closing the final chapter in the monastic occupation of the island which had begun almost exactly nine hundred years before.

With the closure of the priory, the buildings and associated lands remained initially in the control of the See of Durham and they were leased to Thomas Sparke, the last prior. The property came under Crown control when it was sub-let to the King.

The story up to the nineteenth century is one of collapse and decay. The lead was removed from the roofs around 1613 and the structures gradually fell down (**52** and **53**). By 1820 most of the nave and central tower had collapsed and much stone was robbed for building on the island.

However, in this period the Selby family gained possession of the site and so began a phase of clearance and repair of the ruins. In spite of this the west front of the priory collapsed in 1850 and had to be carefully and expensively rebuilt by the Crown (**54**).

In 1887–9 Sir William Crossman excavated the monastic building to produce the above-ground remains which survive today (**55**). At the present time the priory is one of English Heritage's most popular properties.

7

The early medieval settlement at Green Shiel

The most exciting result of the recent programme of research on Lindisfarne has been the discovery and excavation of a well-preserved settlement of the early medieval period, in a part of the Nature Reserve known as Green Shiel, in the sand dunes close to the North Shore. Very few rural settlements of this date have been recognized in northern England and the site fills an important gap, not simply in our understanding of the settlement history of the island, but of the region as a whole. The buildings of the settlement were abandoned and covered by dunes after the original occupation, and so there has been no contamination of the archaeological deposits with material from later periods.

The site was first identified in the middle of the nineteenth century as a result of the expansion of industry on the island. Workmen constructing a waggonway from the limekilns in the dunes came upon some recently exposed ruined stone buildings 'near to that part of Holy Island where the links and sandhills, called the Snook, are united to the enclosed and cultivated part of the island' which they proceeded to quarry for material for the track. In the course of the work two Anglo-Saxon coins were found a short distance to the south, both ninth-century Northumbrian and of a type known as a styca. John Selby, who was then the major landlord on Lindisfarne, published a short note about the discovery in a local journal which dealt with antiquarian findings. He

commented on the possible connection between the coins and the buildings, but his observations were never seriously noted by others and the site was forgotten. The waggonway in its turn was abandoned and is now partly covered by the dunes, but the site has remained exposed in an open, flat area between the foreshore and the main band of dunes, known as the Green Shiel, from which it takes its name.

The visitor to Green Shiel today will see some low walls, overgrown in many places with coarse grass. Careful observation reveals that these form a group of structures. Although the overall plan of the settlement was not clear before the excavation it is now fairly well understood. At least five long narrow buildings are visible, connected with each other to form a cross-shaped plan (**56**). Two early modern stone trackways can also be seen, crossing the shiel at either end of the site, although their course through the dunes to the kilns is now obscured by the sand dunes.

Today, the settlement appears to be in an isolated and marginal location (**57**) but the present surroundings are misleading: the modern dune system had no place in the early medieval landscape. When the concealing cover of the sand hills is lifted it can be seen that the position of the site was carefully chosen, to maximize the area of arable land available. As **colour plate 3** shows, the buildings are sited between the beach and the clay cliff which would have formed the limit of the cultivated land.

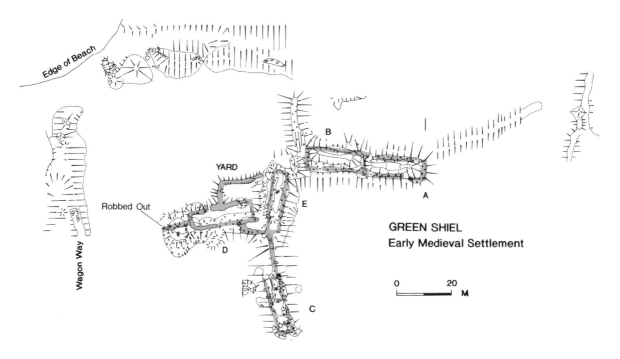

56 *Plan of the buildings at Green Shiel incorporating data from field survey and excavation* (P. Dunn; English Heritage).

The buildings were rediscovered in 1980 during preliminary fieldwork. It would have been rash to accept Selby's premise that the workmen had found an Anglo-Saxon settlement on the basis of his evidence alone, the ruins could have been medieval or even post-medieval dwellings associated with salmon fishing activities on the North Shore. The name 'Coves Cross' appears on the Speed Map of 1610 (see **10**) just where the Green Shiel site is now, and although this might simply have referred to a purely topographic feature, it hinted that the site formed an identifiable component of the post-medieval landscape. The first priority was therefore to date the site, and to this end a geophysical survey was carried out in the hope of perhaps finding a hearth, which could be dated by remanent magnetism, or alternatively some charcoal, for which a radiocarbon date could be obtained. The magnetometer produced a high reading inside the easternmost building (A), near the midpoint of the south wall, and a small area of about 5m × 4m (16½ft × 13ft) was excavated around this point. No hearth was found, but the cause of the readings nonetheless provided the key dating which we sought. It was an Anglo-Saxon spearhead of the late ninth or early tenth century (see **66**(6)), lying in the sand a few centimetres below the surface.

A long-term programme of excavation began at the site in 1985 and is not yet finished, but three of the buildings have now been completely excavated (A, B and C on the plan) and a fourth (D) has been partly investigated. Their state of preservation is variable: the makers of the waggonways clearly removed substantial quantities of material, especially from the western part of the site, and a thousand years of strong winds have scoured out many of the archaeological layers. The reconstruction drawing (**colour plate 12**) gives some impression of how the settlement would have appeared when it was occupied, viewed from the north-west. It is based on archaeological evidence but much of the detail of the standing structures is conjectural. The position of windows or the precise pitch of the roofs, for

57 *Green Shiel in its setting* (RCHM).

example, are not known. It can be fairly safe-ly assumed that the open spaces between the buildings were used in some way, and they have been reconstructed as fenced yards, but small trial pits have failed to reveal any

archaeological features, which may have been scoured out by the wind.

The buildings

At the eastern end of the site is a range of two buildings, A and B, running parallel with the shore (**58**). Archaeologically, these were similar

GREEN SHIEL

BUILDING B

Heavily Robbed Out

Heavily Robbed Out

Shattered Slab
?Entrance

Large Slab

Heavily Robbed Out

Post hole

Heavily Robbed Out

Shattered Slab

N

BUILDING A

Heavily Robbed Out

Drain

Internal Paving Slabs
External Paving Slabs
Stone Hole

0

10

N

M

58 *Plan of Buildings A and B after excavation.*

E

C

B

A

METRES 5

5

0

5

10

59 *Plan of Building C after excavation.*

60 *Reconstruction of interior of Building C, Green Shiel* (P. Dunn; English Heritage).

in plan in many respects, although Building A is considerably better preserved. They were internally divided into two areas, with some flat paving at the eastern end and at least one doorway in the south wall, opening on to the shiel. One end may have been used for animals or the storage of agricultural produce, and the other as a dwelling area, reflecting the divisions

of later medieval peasant long houses, although without the cross-passage which is a typical feature of these later structures.

Immediately to the west of these is a pair of similar structures (D and E) grouped around a stone-walled yard. Excavation in this area is as yet limited, but we have interpreted them as a barn and a house. The southernmost building (C) (**59**) is linked to the yard complex by a well-built stone wall. This building was divided internally into a number of compartments,

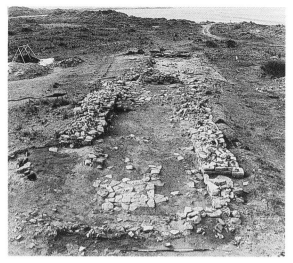

61 *Building A in the course of investigation.*

62 *The west end of building A showing partition wall and flooring.*

and was probably used as a byre (**60**). Excavation has provided further details about individual structures, which enhances our understanding of how they related to each other, and also how they might have been used.

Building A was partly excavated in 1984 and fully investigated in 1988–92 (**61**). This had no less than four doorways, with two in each of the long walls, although not all of these were in use at the same time. The north-west doorway was part of the original construction, but was clearly blocked-up while the building was still in use. The western entrance in the south

wall has a more extensive area of external paving, arranged radially, which showed considerable signs of wear. Just outside the eastern entrance in the south wall was a stone-capped channel, which looked like a drain, although it could never have functioned effectively in this respect as the bottom was unlined and any effluent would simply have soaked into the underlying sand. Excavation revealed that there were at least two distinct phases of use at the west end of the building. In the earliest period, it had been fairly carefully floored with large flat limestone slabs (**62**). After a period of disuse, when clean, blown sand had partly covered this floor and there had been some rubble collapse, another, rather cruder, paved floor was laid down. A hearth was found in the middle of the floor; among the associated burnt material was a pile of hazelnut shells.

The floor levels of Building B were stepped down from Building A, and the south wall was partly terraced into the surrounding sand. The two buildings are separated by a solid gable wall so there was no direct communication between them. The position of the entrances in this building could only be inferred, because the walls had been extensively robbed. A large red sandstone slab, similar to those used in the doorways of Building A, was found just outside the western end of the south wall, and probably indicates a single doorway on this side of the building. There were no entrances in either of the gable walls, and no positive signs of any entrance in the north wall, but this was very badly robbed and almost without facing stones (**colour plate 11**).

Building C, the southernmost building (see **59** and **colour plate 10**) was the first to be fully explored. As with the other structures, there was more than one entrance, this time one in the northern gable wall and another at the midpoint of the eastern wall. It is possible that this was a cross-passage, with another entrance in the western wall at the same point, but unfortunately the stones from this part of the west wall had been mostly robbed away.

The entrance in the northern gable wall opened into a paved, funnel-shaped passage which led directly into a series of compartments. The first compartment could only be entered from the second; all of the others were entered via a corridor running along the western wall. The partition walls had clearly been inserted as a secondary stage in the construction of the structure. Some of the rooms were paved with large flat slabs. There was no sign of a hearth inside the building, and it is therefore unlikely that it was used as a dwelling-house.

The wall at the west end of the site was not visible before excavation, and its abrupt termination was probably the work of the waggonway builders. It is possible that the waggonway itself conceals the western limit of the site. The wall is rather narrow and it was probably part of an enclosure attached to the western building (D) (**63**). Building D has a wide entrance on the northern side, into which some massive building stones have fallen; as with the

other buildings there is some internal stone paving.

Building techniques

The nearby beach seems to have been the source of the building stone; the walling is mostly made from the limestone outcrop along the foreshore, presumably deliberately quarried at low tide, but some large rounded beach pebbles were also used. The walls make use of some fairly massive stones but are otherwise rather crudely constructed. The outer faces of the external walls are built of roughly shaped, rectangular blocks, separated by a rubble infill. There is no trace of mortar or clay bonding in any of the excavated walls, but it is possible that gaps in the stones may have been packed with turves or other vegetal filling which has since disappeared. There was no attempt to build in a regular manner; as the drawn plans suggest, the stonework is irregularly coursed, of variable width and by no means always laid in a straight line. The outer walls were generally broad (up to 2m (6½ ft) in width) which may

63 *The western enclosure wall and Buildings D and E.*

64 *Building B in the course of excavation.*

65 *Penny of Aethelred of Wessex.*

have offered some structural compensation for the rather haphazard construction techniques.

Building B provided the best evidence of how the structures were roofed. A line of three post-holes was discovered running down the centre of the building, indicating that it had been provided with a pitched roof supported by a line of central posts (64). There were no indications of post-holes in Building C; the posts here may have been supported by padstones rather than placed in pits. A number of odd paving stones were found along the centre of the building which could have served this purpose. It seems probable that all of the roofs were supported by central posts, rather than two rows in an aisled plan.

Finds

The excavation is a research project rather than a rescue dig and all of the sand removed has been carefully sieved. In spite of this policy, relatively few objects have been found. Pottery, usually the commonest archaeological artefact, is entirely missing; it was extensively used in eastern and southern England at this time, but much of Northumberland seems to have managed without it from the end of the Roman period until the Norman Conquest. In its absence domestic containers of wood or other organic materials would have been used, but these have left no trace in the sandy soil. Food refuse in the form of animal, bird and fish bone is reasonably abundant, as are the remains of limpets and winkles, which may have been used for bait.

If the two coins discovered in the last century are taken into account, a total of 19 coin finds has been made. One of these is a silver penny of Aethelred of Wessex (866–71), the immediate predecessor of Alfred the Great (65); all the others are examples of the small copper coins known as stycas, which were issued in the name of various Northumbrian kings and Archbishops of York in the course of the ninth century. The coins were found at a number of different places in and around Buildings A, C and D, and are interesting not simply as dating evidence, but also as an indicator of monetary exchange.

The Northumbrian styca coinage contains very little precious metal. While this can be taken as a sign of its low value, it does mean that it could be used for small-scale commercial transactions such as might have occurred between individuals or separate households at Green Shiel. It is admittedly by no means clear

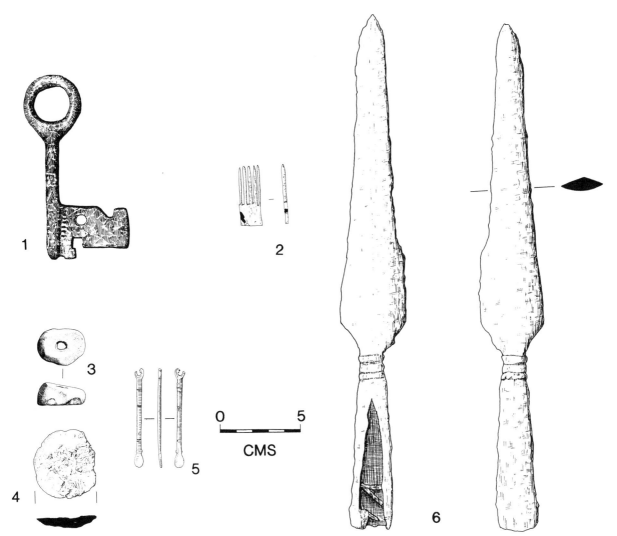

66 *Finds from Green Shiel: 1 Iron Key; 2 fragment of bone comb; 3 amber bead; 4 lead;*
5 copper alloy binding strip; 6 Anglo-Saxon spearhead

that stycas were in fact widely used in this way in the countryside, but examples have been found on other rural sites of the period. Seven of the coins were found within a couple of metres of each other, just to the south of Building D in an area much disturbed by rabbits. These may represent a small hoard; but it is clear from the scattered distribution of the other coins that we are not generally dealing with hoarded money, but with casual losses in the course of exchange.

A number of the other finds discovered are illustrated in **66**; some of which are on display in Lindisfarne Museum. The spearhead, found in the first season, is probably the most interesting object. This has a shallow midrib and a split socket, with a double roll moulding at the base of the blade and is an Anglo-Saxon rather than a Viking weapon. A large iron key indicates the need for security at the site; a small strip of bronze may have been part of an ornament applied to a wooden or leather object. A single amber bead from the floor of Building C is the only personal ornament found. Animal bone is well preserved from the site, but the two fragments of bone comb are the only

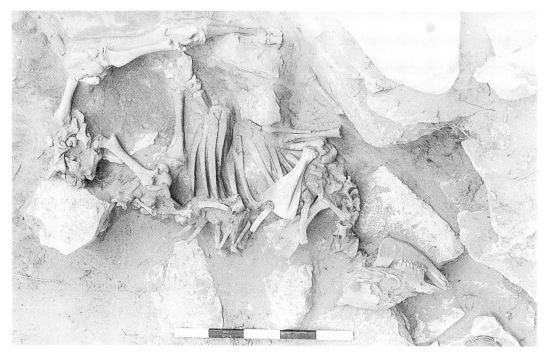

67 *Cow burial in Building C.*

preserved bone artefacts. Other finds include two honestones and a couple of small iron knives. Some industrial activity is shown by the presence of a small amount of iron smithing slag, in and around Buildings C and D, and lead droplets and a circular pat of lead which were recovered from the second phase of activity at Building A.

Several complete cattle carcases have been found in the interior of the houses. These include two animals which were buried together in a pit at the east end of Building A, and another in a pit in the western part of the same building. Another complete skeleton was found immediately inside the south-west doorway: this seems to have been dumped on the surface rather than buried. No carcases were found in Building B, but there were two in Building C, one adult animal in a pit in the southernmost compartment and another calf by the entrance to this compartment (**67**), which again appeared to have been simply dumped. It is not unknown for farmers to bury dead cattle where they die, but it seems most improbable that the dumped carcases were simply left *in situ* when the buildings were still in use. The

cattle probably date from a period after the abandonment of the settlement, though probably not very long after, as they all seem to underlie any rubble collapse, which suggests that the buildings were still standing. There is a considerable amount of butchered cattle bone from the site which is more certainly related to its occupation. The age and sex of the animals indicates that the cattle economy was based principally on dairying.

Among the general bone refuse from different parts of the site are the remains of some marine mammals – seals and a whale – which may have been stranded on the nearby shore. The bones of deer and a range of fish provide evidence of hunting and fishing. The bird bone includes that of the now extinct Great Auk; it was last spotted on the Northumbrian coast towards the end of the eighteenth century.

Green Shiel in its setting

The nature of the settlement at Green Shiel remains to be considered. The population was clearly smaller than that of a village, but greater than a single nuclear family – perhaps two or three households lived at the site. These were more or less self-sufficient, at least where the basic necessities of life were concerned. If the general poverty of finds is any indication, it was not an affluent community, but it did make use of coinage, so clearly there was some opportunity for trade and exchange within the region. The comb fragments, the amber bead and the little bronze strip would have been acquired from elsewhere, perhaps ultimately from a trading centre such as York.

Green Shiel's connection with the Anglo-Saxon monastery is uncertain. There is nothing to suggest that the inhabitants followed a monastic way of life, and it seems best to view it as an ordinary, secular settlement. The evidence of the finds indicates that it was occupied in the middle and later part of the ninth century, before the island was finally abandoned by the monastic community, but as already noted, the monks left Lindisfarne and went to Norham for an unknown length of time in the mid-ninth century. The beginnings of the site may lie in this period of abandonment. It is possible that the site was deserted at the time of the last recorded Viking raid in 875 or shortly afterwards.

The settlement seems to have been fairly short-lived; although there is some evidence for remodelling and refurbishment, the occupation of the site may only have lasted for a generation. Interestingly, this feature is shared by the other, earlier rural settlements in the area and suggests that the pattern of rural settlement was fairly mobile. It is not known whether Green Shiel would have been the only settlement on Lindisfarne in the later ninth century, but this seems unlikely. Population density was generally low in this period but it was almost certainly on the increase, and given the availability of marine resources the island could certainly have supported a few more households. The location of these is now a matter of guesswork, but there might have been another settlement within the abandoned monastery on the site of Holy Island village, and possibly another somewhere in the north-eastern part of the island. It is tempting to reconstruct a pattern of small clusters of households ringing

the arable and pasture lands of the island, which coalesced or were transplanted in Norman times to the site of the present village; Green Shiel would have been one node in this pattern. The present pattern of nucleated villages with open fields is almost certainly a product of the period immediately after the Norman Conquest in this area; before this, rural settlements would have been dispersed throughout the landscape, although there may have been some communal agricultural activity.

Although the settlements themselves were mobile, the organizational framework of the landscape suggests great continuity. The island would have remained part of a large estate and still the property of the wandering Cuthbert community. These early estates usually covered large areas and contained within them a wide range of upland and lowland resources. In addition to farm products, the settlement of Green Shiel may have provided more specialized marine produce.

A general economic context can be provided, but it is less easy to identify the cultural affinities of the buildings themselves. A number of settlement sites have been identified in the region which can be dated to the early Anglo-Saxon period (c. 550–650) but these seem to represent very different building traditions (see 1). On the slopes of Yeavering Bell, an extensive settlement identified with *Ad Gefrin*, the royal estate centre where Paulinus preached to King Edwin's people, has been excavated, and similar sites are known at Sprouston and Milfield, which may likewise have been the centres of estates. At these sites large halls are associated with other buildings which probably served a public function; in the case of Yeavering, a church and a curious structure resembling an open theatre have been recognized. Perhaps more typical of ordinary rural farmsteads are the sites at Thirlings and New Bewick; at Thirlings a group of rectangular timber halls with ancillary buildings dating to the late sixth century has been uncovered, while at New Bewick, a sunken building, of the type known as a *grüben-*

haus, has been excavated. Although the scale of construction varies, these buildings from northern Northumbria are part of a widespread, related tradition of timber building which seems to have used similar constructional techniques, proportions and units of measurement, and which is represented in many other areas of Anglo-Saxon England. The buildings at Green Shiel thus make a substantial break with earlier regional traditions, both in terms of the building materials used and the proportions and plans of the structures. How did this arise?

Within the kingdom of Northumbria, a small number of sites have been identified, more closely contemporary with Green Shiel, which make use of stone for building, at Simy Folds in Teesdale, Gauber High Pasture, Ribblehead and Bryant's Gill, Kentmere in the Lake District (see **1**). All these settlements are in what would now be considered marginal areas, where there is substantial evidence of Scandinavian settlement in the ninth and tenth centuries, and they are often viewed as the homes of new colonizers who introduced their own building tradition. Comprehensive archaeological information is not available, but these sites usually appear to be isolated settlements; Simy Folds may consist of a group of three homesteads. Although they make use of the same building materials, however, they do not compare very closely in structural detail, and there are other reasons why it is unlikely that the ninth-century inhabitants of Lindisfarne would have drawn on a Scandinavian tradition. Firstly, the coin evidence indicates that the buildings at Green Shiel are earlier than the period of Scandinavian colonization. In eastern England this followed on from the arrival of the Great Army and the capture of York in 867, and in north-west England it seems to have been even later. Secondly, although it is

known that part of the Army was encamped on the Tyne in 875 there is no evidence that Scandinavian settlers penetrated or colonized north of this: in both eastern England and Cumbria, extensive Scandinavian settlement is evidenced by the abundance of place-names of Scandinavian origin, which are not found north of the Tyne.

It is possible that the move to building in stone has nothing to do with the ethnic origins of the islanders. Although secular dwellings were generally built in timber, the use of stone for monastic buildings and churches was already familiar to Northumbrians in this period, and the decision to utilize the local rock-outcrops may represent not so much a constructional innovation as a pragmatic adaptation, to exploit available raw materials. As long as the basic organization of the community's estate remained in place, items such as the large timbers needed to continue building in the local tradition could have been provided from areas of managed woodland on the mainland. St Cuthbert's coffin was made from just such an oak, acquired from a well-maintained forest.

The troubled times of the ninth century may have resulted in some breakdown of the internal organization of the estate which supported the Anglo-Saxon monastery, leaving the island community much more dependent on their own resources. It may have become increasingly difficult to obtain large structural timbers, and the islanders therefore turned to the easily quarried limestone outcrops on the North Shore for their raw materials. Ironically, it is this decision to abandon the traditional materials which has resulted in the survival of the farmstead into modern times, offering a rare insight into the lives and customs of the ordinary rural population.

8

The castle and the island fortifications

Lindisfarne Castle (**68**), now part of the National Trust, is today one of the island's dominant features. Viewed from the priory its striking setting more than compensates for its diminutive size, and few visitors can resist the temptation to capture it on postcard or film. Although it seems to belong more to a fairytale than a system of fortification, it has had an interesting and varied history, and its present guise as an elegant Edwardian weekend residence is only the most recent of many transformations.

Northumberland is rightly famous for its many magnificent medieval castles, some ruinous, like nearby Norham, Warkworth and Dunstanburgh; some like Bamburgh now transformed into imposing stately homes. Such castles were the products of the many centuries of baronial conflict and border warfare, but the traces of these conflicts on Lindisfarne must be looked for in the priory walls. There was no medieval seigneurial residence on the island, and the castle and its much more neglected sister fortification, the small enclosed blockhouse known as Osborne's Fort on the Heugh at Steel End (**69**) were both post-medieval constructions. The latter, sadly now in ruins, is in its own way just as interesting but more enigmatic than the better-known structure on the Castle Rock. The medieval monastic community had occasional need of defences, as already noted, but the first serious attempts at erecting independent military fortification on the island were made in the 1530s.

The construction of military forts to protect the harbour at Holy Island needs to be explained in terms of perceived threats to the realm, rather than concern about the welfare of the villagers or any particular importance which was attached to the island itself. Relations with the Scots had been problematic for centuries, and the Anglo-Scottish border had seen major rearrangements in the recent

68 *A general view of Holy Island Castle from the south-west.*

69 *Osborne's Fort at the east end of the Heugh.*

past. The town of Berwick-upon-Tweed, the only major settlement in the immediate vicinity, had passed into English control as recently as 1482. It turned out to be a permanent arrangement, but this outcome might have seemed far from inevitable in the mid-sixteenth century. Henry VIII might well have viewed conflict in the Borders as endemic and incurable.

Quite apart from the issue of local or regional theatres of conflict, however, was the highly problematic question of Henry's own sovereignty, and that of his successors. His will and desire was to be succeeded by his own children, but his complex marital arrangements and his own actions gave plenty of ground to those who wished to query the legitimate title of his direct heirs. The progeny of his sister Margaret, who had married the King of Scots in 1503, were specifically excluded from the English succession but a Scottish threat to the English throne

lurked constantly over the horizon and had resulted in invasion in 1513. After his excommunication by the Pope in 1538, Henry had cause also to fear attack from the Continent. His first response was to carry out a review of his coastal defences, and this in turn led to the investment of substantial sums in the defence of the northern border, to discourage both local conflict and the possibility of a major Scottish attack on his kingdom. These changes were all the more necessary as the use of artillery became the norm in military encounters. Repairs to existing fortifications and defences at Berwick, Carlisle, Wark, Bamburgh and Alnwick were immediately set in hand.

Using attack as a form of defence, Henry's troops invaded southern Scotland in 1542, 1544 and 1547. The threat from Scotland remained throughout the reigns of his children, Edward, Mary and Elizabeth, and necessitated the maintenance of regular garrisons in the region. A series of Acts of Parliament was passed in these reigns to make better provision for the cost of repairs to the northern defences, but there was a constant struggle to balance the cost of building strong defences against the equally onerous cost of maintaining large and expensive garrisons. The elaborate Italianate Elizabethan fortifications of Berwick-upon-Tweed, begun under Queen Mary, were in the forefront of contemporary military design but cost nearly £130,000 to construct, a staggering amount at the time, and ten times larger than the expenditure on any other military building of Elizabeth's reign.

By comparison, the fortification of Lindisfarne was a fairly modest affair. As early as 1531, when Christopher Kemp was appointed Controller of Berwick, we know that one Francis Pawne had charge of buildings owned or leased by the Crown on Lindisfarne. Given its proximity to the Scottish border and the town of Berwick, and also its sheltered harbour, the island was an obvious choice as a base for the landing of soldiers and supplies, and the letters and papers of Henry VIII show that Lindisfarne was used for just this purpose in 1523–4 and again in the period 1542–4. However, it was not until the reign of Edward VI that the Crown gained full control of all of the buildings within the boundaries of the priory and in the village.

In 1539 an Order in Council decreed that all 'Havens should be fensed with bulwarks and blockehouses against the scots' and it is possible that work began in response to this somewhere on the island. However, it is more probable that construction began properly in August 1542, when the King ordered the Earl of Rutland to send workmen from Berwick to Lindisfarne and to construct two earthen bulwarks 'thone to be set in such a place as woll beate the rode, thother in the most propice place to defende the Ilande'. The same order mentions men and ordnance to defend both the island and 'the rode' – the main seaway in and out of the harbour. Work continued throughout the autumn of that year but it was

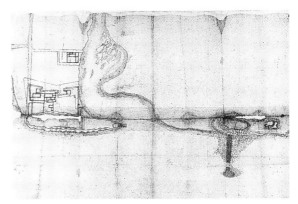

70 *Plan of Holy Island fortifications in 1548 showing the proposed fortifications around the priory and parish church* (PRO, MPF 369).

slow and the ordnance was in short supply. By 1544, however, the fortifications had suffered setbacks and were reported as being out of repair. The situation was rescued by the Earl of Shrewsbury, who sent the master mason from Berwick and who was thanked by the Privy Council for his efforts. By May of 1545, at the height of one of several border panics, when Lindisfarne was again visited by Berwick's master mason, Thomas Gower, in the company of engineers sent by the Privy Council, the defences were found to be much decayed and very badly sited with respect to defensive capabilities. A new defence was immediately erected 'towardes the haven's mouth upon a rock callid bolstress heugh' and it was ready to be armed and manned. By 1545, three separate sites on the island had had defensive earthworks built on them, and there is great debate as to just where these were located. It is possible that the present castle was not constructed at this time. A plan of 1548 shows that Beblowe (or Biblaw(e)) had nothing on it except a beacon, but other features are of more than passing interest (**70**). For instance, the drawing shows that there was an intention to defend the area around the priory with very elaborate work similar in design to some of the fortifications at Berwick. The detailed description suggests that the costs of this would have been prohibitive, however.

Another interesting feature is the small circular banked enclosure that is visible on the end of the Heugh in the area that was later to be dominated by Osborne's Fort. This may be all that is left of the bulwark constructed by Gower on his visit in 1545. Here recent fieldwork may provide some relevant if tenuous information. There is a substantial layer of pebbles and sand overlying the possibly prehistoric layers eroding at the end of the Heugh (see **17**). Seen in section this has the appearance of a truncated bank, and although it is possible that this is a later storm beach deposit, it is also feasible that it is the much-reduced remains of the feature recorded on the 1548 plan.

The emplacement at the east end of the Castle Rock also deserves some comment in this context. Unfortunately no real structural details are visible now, and the construction of the limekilns in the 1860s clearly destroyed much of the rock in this area. The 1548 drawing indicates that the defence work was built on two levels and consisted of three small platforms and a rectangular blockhouse. Two entrances from outside the perimeter are visible on the western side of the defences, one on each level. All of this is very interesting in terms of the general history of military involvement on the island, but it does not help us to pin down the date for the construction of the castle. On the basis of documents which attest further spending on military building on the island in 1548–9, and the fact that the fort of Beblowe is mentioned in Sir Robert Bowes' work, *A Book of the State of the Frontiers and Marches between England and Scotland* in 1550, it would appear that this was probably about 1549.

Bowes had some radical suggestions for the enhancement of the fort:

The fort of Beblowe, within the Holy Island, lyeth very well for the defence of the Haven theire; and if there were about the lower part thereof made a ring, with bulwarks to flank the same, the ditch whereabout might be easily watered toward the land. And then I

think the said fort were very strong and stood for good purpose both for the defence of the forte and the annoyance of the enemies, if they did arrive in any other part of that island...

The proposed moat was never built but Bowes was under no illusion about the military importance of Lindisfarne at this time:

The Holy Island is also a place much necessarye to be defended and preserved for there is a harborough sufficient for a great range of shippes to rest safely in and very aptly for the warrs towards Scotland...

This was a point reiterated by no less a person than Queen Elizabeth I in a letter dated 1569, when she put Lord Hundson 'in remembrance of Holy Island, the importance of the place being as such as cannot be too wareley looked into'. This was not before Sir Richard Lee in an inspection of northern defences dated 1565 noted that:

Biblawe...ys nothinge but a high rock and a plattforame made on the toppe, and a vamure therof being of turf which ys now consumed away, by which means ther ys no man able to stand on the plattforame to do any searvyce nere wherfore yt lyes so open.

The garrison in 1559 consisted of a captain (non-resident), two master gunners who were paid a shilling a day, one master's mate paid 10d a day and 20 soldiers paid 8d a day. The complement remained at this strength for at least another 80 years.

In 1550 there was peace in the north and the island seems to have lost some of its strategic importance, but by 1557, the then captain, Sir William Read, was fighting his corner with great vigour in an effort to have the fortifications on the island maintained. By 1567 £500 had been spent in building walls twelve feet high at the site and by 1571 it seems that the basic shape of the castle as we now know it was completed. The structure is orientated roughly east–west along the whin-sill ridge of Biblaw. It is broadly oval in shape and measures *c.* 68m (220ft) along its long axis. The internal arrangements of the central range of barracks/dwelling structures were totally remodelled by Sir Edwin Lutyens (see below), but the upper and lower battery or gun platforms at the east and west ends remain largely in their original form. The entrance to the castle is on the southern, seaward side, approached by a steep ramp. The walls on the north side are sheer with the cliff. The lower battery retains two fine bastion-like gun emplacements, built into the perimeter wall.

In the late 1560s and early 1570s some £1691 3s $\frac{1}{2}$d was spent on construction at the site and up to 1599 the fortifications and their associated structures on both the Farne Islands and Lindisfarne received regular maintenance.

When James VI of Scotland became also James I of England on the death of Elizabeth I in 1601, more lasting peace came to the north and the military importance of the castle and the harbour decreased substantially. However, the garrison was still maintained and there is ample evidence in the parish registers for the pattern of marriages, births and deaths among the soldier population. For example, the entries for May to July 1639 record some thirty soldiers buried, and the July entries close with the general statement that 'about this tyme were sundrie sogers buryed'. On the happier side there are many records of the birth of children to the soldiers of the castle.

The castle was not without its characters in this period, most notably the governor just before the middle years of the seventeenth century, one Captain Rugge, by repute a generous man with a huge bottle nose. This same Rugge wrote a rhyming letter to King Charles I asking for the settling-up of eighteen months' back pay. The poem gives some insight into the kind of character that was needed to be stationed in what might have been seen at the time as a military backwater. Rugge signed himself as

The great Commander of the Cormorants
The Geese and Ganders of these Hallowed lands.

Rugge was still owed money when he handed his command over to the Parliamentary forces in 1645. Indeed, he died before the debt was settled, and a grant of money from Parliament in recognition of his services was left to his daughter in his will. His successor, Colonel Shaftoe, had similar problems in obtaining his pay.

With northern developments in the Civil War, Holy Island Castle again became a focus of military interest. Throughout the war it held out for the Parliamentary side, and two years after the replacement of Captain Rugge, when Berwick fell to the Royalists, the then commander, Captain Batton, stood firm when asked to surrender by Sir Marmaduke Langdale. It is obvious from the offer made to Batton, namely that the King's side would make good his arrears of pay if he agreed to change sides and administer the castle for the Royalists, that life was still hard for the commander and men of this northern outpost. To his credit, and to the approbation of a grateful Parliament, Batton refused to turn his coat.

A year later after a siege lasting six weeks which made life very hard for both commander and garrison, he had still not received any money. The situation was relieved by soldiers bringing 'necessaries' to the island; but the following year the situation seems to have been equality as bad. Batton had to send his wife with urgent dispatches to Newcastle to seek relief for the trapped garrison. This relief came in the form of troops led by a Major Meyer who brought six months' supplies with them but still no money!

Even under all of this stress the round of births, deaths and marriages still went on on the island. The parish register records that on 24 August 1648 a baby girl christened Marie was born to one Heughe Dowglas 'a gunner, shot in the castle'. One can only speculate as to the sort of conditions into which the little girl was born.

After the second relief, things seemed to quieten down for the defenders of the castle and as the years wore on the record tells us more of rebuilding and other maintenance work than heroic deeds. A surviving letter of 15 October 1687 gives some indication of the living conditions of the men stationed on Lindisfarne at this time. The letter was written by William Selby and Gilbert Orde, bailiffs of the Corporation of the Island, to Lord Dartmouth. Their aim was to acquaint his lordship with the hardship the garrison faced, billeted as it was on very poor people in the village, and they asked that 'twelve beds may be placed in the castle, so that the poorer sort of inhabitant may be eased, and the soldiers not forced to lie in that cold place upon straw, very slenderly covered'. It would seem that even in times of peace the life of a soldier on Lindisfarne was fairly uncomfortable!

Further documentation shows that although the castle was no longer of any great military significance in the latter part of the seventeenth century it still had its fair share of visits from distinguished persons. One such document is an account of gunpowder used and numbers of guns fired for both the castle and Osborne's Fort for the period 29 May 1679 to 19 August 1681. The cannon seems to have been fired off at the slightest opportunity. The visitors included 'The Honourable Lord Rosseth, then Chancelor of Scotland' (11 July 1679); the Governor of Berwick (18 July 1679); 'Sir Ralph Delavall and his Ladye and other persons of quallytye' (1 August 1679) and a range of other 'lesser persons' over the period. Salutes were also fired at the drinking of the King's health, the health of the Duke of York, to celebrate St George's Day, Guy Fawkes Day, Charles II's birthday and Restoration, and on a host of other occasions.

The only other military event in which the castle figures, if indeed it can properly be considered such, is its capture in 1715 by two supporters of the Young Pretender. Guns in the castle were fired in anger on this occasion against the rightful occupiers of the building. The story of this capture is still a part of island lore, and invariably features in guided tours of the building.

The heroes, or villains, of the hour were one Launcelot Errington and his nephew, Mark Errington. Errington senior was the captain of a ship which had put into the harbour of Lindisfarne, carrying a cargo of salt, brandy and other goods. The younger Errington was the mate of this vessel. The older man gained access to the castle on the pretence of having his beard shaved by the master gunner, Samuel Phillipson, who worked as a barber in his spare time, perhaps a form of compensation for the irregularity of his pay. After his shave Errington left the castle but returned immediately, claiming that he had lost his watch key. His nephew also gained access at this time and the two men then rounded on the master gunner with pistols. They then proclaimed the castle as their own, evicting Phillipson and another member of the garrison, the only occupants, and barring the door.

The garrison was only half its normal strength of fourteen at the time; a popular though false rumour claimed that the Erringtons had made the soldiers drunk before they carried out their attack. After unfurling the Pretender's standard and firing cannon shots towards the shore, probably as a signal to reinforcements that never materialized, the captors cursed and roundly abused the members of the garrison, who were attempting to return inside. Shots were exchanged in this encounter and finally one of the soldiers, Francis Amos, a corporal in the Hon. Piercy Kirk's Regiment of Foot, managed to get to Berwick and give the news of the castle's capture to Colonel Layton, the commanding officer in the town. He set out with a party which included Amos. The fortress was duly retaken with a minimum of fuss and the two intruders were made prisoner. Launcelot Errington was wounded in the process

71 *Holy Island Castle: kitchen* (National Trust).

and the two would-be rebels were escorted to Berwick and kept in custody. However, with the help of several sympathizers in the town they soon escaped. The party which retook the castle was given the king's share of the brandy confiscated from Errington's ship. Various witnesses and participants were sworn before the Mayor of Berwick in the ensuing enquiry, who recounted the details of the affair, vindicating the sobriety of the garrison. Launcelot Errington subsequently went on to a career as a publican in Newcastle.

After this incident the history of the castle is one of gradual decline until its restoration in 1902. The garrison was reduced even further in size and was finally removed in 1819. A detachment of men from the navy occupied it as coastguards in 1841 and the building had become a civilian coastguard station by 1851. It was subsequently used as the headquarters of the Northumberland Artillery Volunteers for a couple of decades, and after this became rapidly ruinous.

Lutyens and the castle

In 1902 Edward Hudson, the founder of the magazine *Country Life* bought what was by then a broken-down shell from the Crown and commissioned Edwin Lutyens to restore it. This marks the beginnings of the modern phases of the castle's use as a country house (**71, 72**). Lutyens had previously designed another house for Hudson, Deanery Hall at Sonning in Berkshire, and at thirty-three he was already one of the most celebrated architects of his generation. By an amazing coincidence, his later career led him to reconstruct the castle on Lambay, another small inshore island north of Dublin,

72 *Holy Island Castle: passageway* (National Trust).

also the site of an early Christian monastery and the scene of the first Viking attack on Ireland.

Lutyens preserved the outer shell of the castle walls, but completely transformed the interior. The kitchen and other shared amenities were located on the lower floor, making new use of what had probably been the ammunition storerooms of the Tudor fort; bedrooms were grouped around the long gallery upstairs. The Upper and Lower Batteries were designed as open spaces within the walled precinct. The Lower Battery is the site of the original cannon platform; the Upper Battery provides wonderful views of both the island and the Northumberland coast.

The main source of inspiration for Lutyens seems to have been early seventeenth-century Dutch interiors, but the fine Romanesque buildings of the north are echoed in the sturdy, round-arched arcade of the entrance hall and in the long gallery. Medieval notes are also struck in Gothic window tracery, the wide fireplaces of the kitchen and dining room, and the cruciform arrow-slits of the west range. The basic decor was simple, even austere: whitewashed walls contrast with herringbone brick floors and massive and solid dark wood furnishings, but are relieved by gleaming brass and simply painted blue-and-white china. The furniture includes many fine sixteenth- and seventeenth-century Flemish pieces but Lutyens also commissioned modern items such as the

Prospect of Holy Island from the west

The Ground Plott of Holy Island vpon the Coaste of Northumberland neere Berwick Surveyd in the yeare one Thousand Sixe Seventy Three

73 *The entrance to Holy Island harbour c. 1670, showing Osborne's Fort and the castle in use.*

74 *Plan of Osborne's Fort in 1742.*

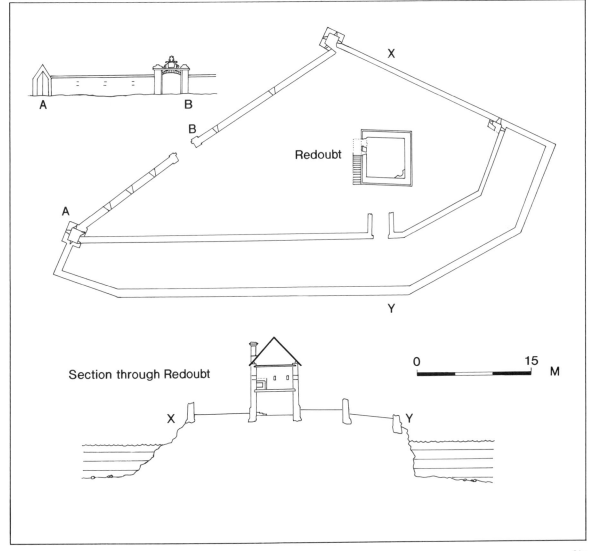

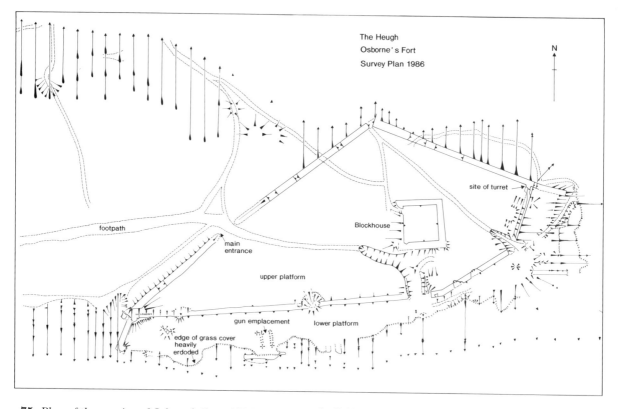

The Heugh
Osborne's Fort
Survey Plan 1986

N

site of turret

Blockhouse

footpath

main
entrance

upper platform

gun emplacement   lower platform

edge of grass cover
heavily
erdoded

75 *Plan of the remains of Osborne's Fort, 1986.*

massive oak dresser in the kitchen and the copper fish-kettles by W. A. S. Benson, a pioneer of the Arts and Crafts movement, which also harmonize beautifully with their setting.

The restored building was intended to serve as a weekend and summer retreat rather than a year-round residence. Lutyens' elegant and efficient use of the circulation areas between rooms and galleries has been widely celebrated, but the limited interior space and restricted number of bedrooms meant that it was not really suitable for large parties; indeed, there was only one bathroom in the original design! Hudson's weekend guests included many of the great and famous, however, including the Prince and Princess of Wales, who stayed there briefly in 1908.

In 1926 Hudson sold the building in its restored state to a London banker named O. T. Falk, who in turn passed it on to another banker, Sir Edward de Stein. In 1944 the building was donated to the National Trust, who still own and maintain the property. De Stein's family remained as tenants until 1968. Lindisfarne Castle has featured in a number of films, including Polanski's *Macbeth* and *Cul de Sac.*

Some mention should also be made of Gertrude Jekyll's walled garden, which is situated opposite the castle north of the rather boggy pasture known as the Stank. This was built about 1911, utilizing an old sheep pen. It was designed as both a flower and vegetable garden, and has recently been restored, using many of the species of the original design. Jekyll, who was easily as distinguished a figure in her own field as Lutyens was in his, co-operated with him on a number of projects, including Lambay and Lindisfarne, and her original plans for the structure and layout still survive.

Osborne's Fort

The remains of this little structure are on the eastern end of the Heugh. It was designed and built by Major Daniel Collingwood and Robert Trollope in 1675. Collingwood's involvement is known through a surviving financial account for the actual construction of the fort; that of Trollope is known from an entry in the Holy Island parish register for 10 April 1675, which records that both Collingwood and Trollope stood as 'Surties' at the baptism of one Ralph Mitchelson. Trollope is described as 'master builder of the forth of Holy Island'.

It is thought that the fort was constructed as a government response to the growing threat of Dutch privateers on the east coast in this period, and a print of the early 1670s (**73**) shows both the castle and the fort when they were still in use; an architect's drawing of it in 1742 also survives (**74**).

The fort as originally planned consisted of a lozenge-shaped enclosure with two levels or platforms, the walls of which were no more than 1.5m (5ft) thick. It also had a central, two-storey redoubt or blockhouse, the upper storey of which was reached by an exterior staircase. No trace of this stairway remains on the surviving ruins, but the height of the upper floor level can be deduced from the joist holes which are still visible in the walls. The lower floor was probably a storeroom of some sort; the upper level would have sheltered the small garrison of on-duty soldiers.

A comparison between the 1742 drawing and a modern survey (**75**) reveals how much damage has been done to the site since the eighteenth century. Most of the lower platform on the seaward side has been washed away, although fragments of the outer walling can still be seen on the rocks. One possible gun emplacement is still visible as a series of depressions in the grass, but even this is rapidly being eroded. Very little now survives of the entranceway through the outer wall which cut off the neck of the promontory, although the drawing indicates that this was originally a fairly impressive affair, surmounted with a coat of arms. Traces of the artillery embrasures in this wall can still be located on the ground, although nothing can now be seen of the northernmost angle-tower. There are still traces of the small tower on the eastern side of the redoubt at the junction of the internal and external walls. Some restoration and conservation work has now been attempted on this interesting little ruin, but it seems likely that it will eventually fall victim to the tides.

9

The island community

In tracing the origins of the village community it should be remembered that while it is not known whether there was a secular population on Lindisfarne before the ninth century, it is improbable that there would have been any settlement separate and independent of the Anglo-Saxon monastery. The monastic rule would have permitted the employment of servants and lay brethren, and it is known that the island cemetery was occasionally used by lay people. Mention has already been made of the eighth-century memorial which bears a woman's name, Osgyth, and Bede recounts the tale of a Northumbrian nobleman who sought the privilege of burial on Lindisfarne for his wife (*Vita Cuthberti*, ch 15). With the departure of the monastic community, however, the island lost much of its focal importance and probably supported a typical, rather lowly, small rural community for a couple of centuries. The settlement at Green Shiel was not occupied for a long period, but the secular population continued to thrive, even after the refoundation of the cell of Durham.

The island community in the Middle Ages

The island may have escaped the devastation of William the Conqueror's troops in 1069–70, as it was here that the monks of Durham sought refuge for the shrine of Cuthbert, but it is difficult to know if the roots of the present village go back this far. There is some evidence that from at least the thirteenth century, there was a concentration of settlement in this area, and it is tempting to see the village as an Anglo-Norman foundation. Very little is known about the secular community from either documents or archaeology.

The medieval parish of Holy Island consisted of a number of separate chapelries – Holy Island, Kyloe, Ancroft and Tweedmouth (**76**). Holy Island chapelry itself consisted of the constableries of Holy Island, and Fenham and Goswick on the mainland; St Mary's parish church would therefore have served a population considerably larger than the actual island community. The priory had control over the living, paying the curate an annual stipend.

The parish church – St Mary's

The monks maintained a certain spiritual exclusiveness and the pastoral needs of the parishioners were attended to in their own parish church, dedicated to St Mary the Virgin, rather than through participation in the services and offices in the priory. Historic sources indicate that a church of some kind was in existence at the end of the eleventh century and reference has already been made to the early features which lie at the core of the present building (see above, Chapter 4).

Like the great majority of English parish churches, the church on Lindisfarne is a composite structure with architectural features of different periods (**77**, **78**). It is an attractive

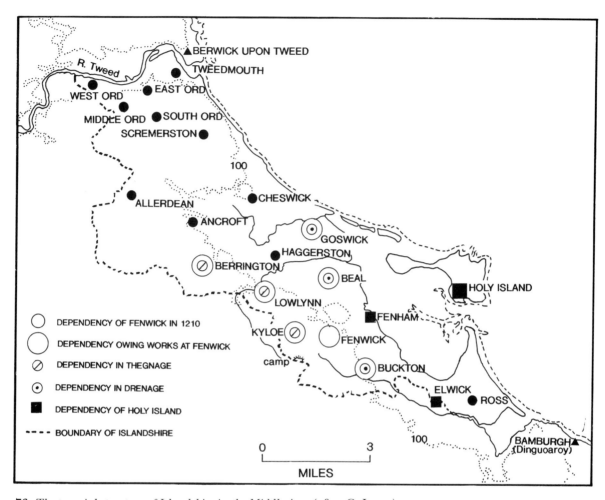

76 *The tenurial structure of Islandshire in the Middle Ages* (after G. Jones).

though unremarkable building, extensively restored in about 1860. Whatever the date of the early features, the first stone church clearly consisted of a nave and chancel with high narrow walls, and in the course of the Middle Ages this building was altered and extended in a number of ways. In the late twelfth century, a north aisle was added and a three-arched arcade inserted between the new aisle and the existing nave. This arcade incorporates an interesting decorative use of contrasting red and light-grey stonework in alternate courses in the arch ribs, which rest on red sandstone columns. Perhaps this reflects the changing availability of building stone or the building programme at the adjacent priory, where the general use of red sand-

stone is limited to the church itself. Later, in the late thirteenth century, the nave seems to have been extended to both the west and south, necessitating the construction of an additional bay in the north arcade as well as a new south aisle. The pointed arches of the south arcade rest on octagonal columns and are not paired with those on the north aisle. The present pointed chancel arch was probably also built at this time, although it is clearly a later insertion in an earlier fabric. The chancel was extended and modified by the construction of a number of new windows, including three single lancets in the east wall of the chancel and the west wall of the nave. A number of other windows in the church are modifications

101

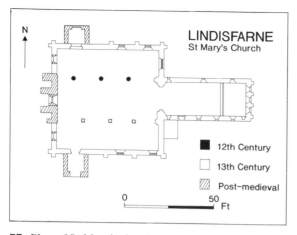

77 *Plan of St Mary's church.*

of the later Middle Ages, although some work dates from the Victorian restoration. There are two windows in the decorated style in the south wall of the south aisle; the walls of the north aisle contain two double and one triple light. The north and south porches, and the bell-cote are post-medieval additions.

These alterations resulted in a church about

78 *St Mary's church from the south.*

twice the size of the original. The larger church could have been a response to an expanding community, to bequests and endowments, to changes in prevailing architectural style, or it may have simply come about because vital repairs became necessary from time to time. Various internal features suggest that the interior space was at least partly divided up into a number of chapels or chantries. There are three aumbreys incorporated in the walling, two in the chancel, and one in the north aisle, and there is a piscina in the south-east angle of the south aisle.

The surrounding churchyard would have been the burial place for the village community, as well as the other parishioners of Holy Island. It is possible that some of the more influential were buried inside the church. Burial within the church became much more common in post-Reformation times, and there are a number of post-medieval commemorative plaques. In 1986, a small excavation was carried out near the centre of the south aisle. This did not produce any architectural evidence of earlier buildings, but it did reveal a large stone-lined

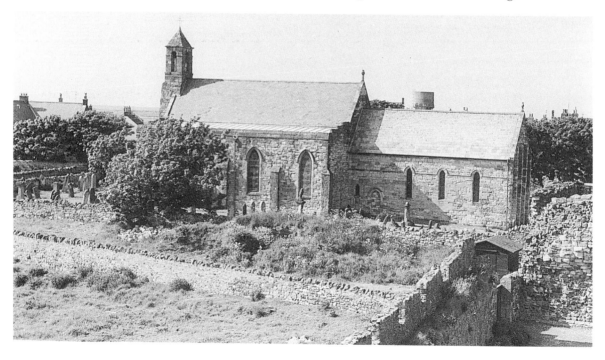

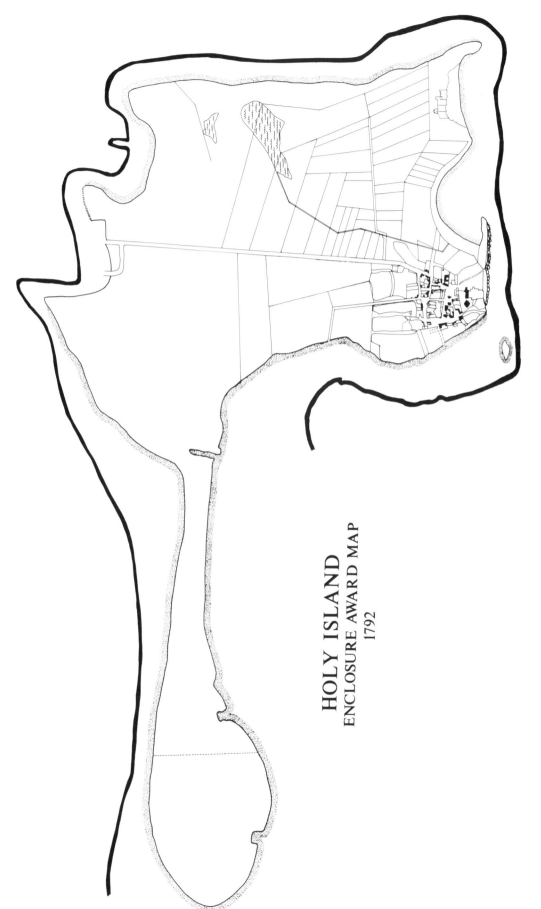

HOLY ISLAND
ENCLOSURE AWARD MAP
1792

79 *The Enclosure of Holy Island, c. 1792.*

burial vault, pre-dating the 1860 restoration, containing the remains of at least eight different individuals. It is likely that there are many similar interments elsewhere in the floor.

The village in the Middle Ages

Documents relating to the priory contain surprisingly little detail about the village, mainly because it is usually impossible to separate information which applies specifically to Lindisfarne from the aggregrated income from different sources which appears in the priory accounts. The monks owned some property on the island, and received the benefits of tithes and other rentals from the local people, but it is difficult to get a clear picture of the size of the population, or the types of industry or farming practised.

Fishing was clearly significant, as the consumption of fish was important to the monastic diet. The earliest surviving account roll of 1326 notes the presence of sixty dried codfish in the priory larder and a succession of later inventories record materials for salting, and stores of lamprey, salmon, haddock, herring, cod and possibly ling. Towards the end of the fourteenth century the monks consciously adopted a policy of investment in the local industry, in the hope of making cash profits. In 1376 the sum of £17 11s was spent on a ship and a boat and in the 1380s expenditure increased considerably, with the purchase of more boats and special herring nets. Wages were paid to groups of up to ten fishermen. The fishing venture continued for a number of decades, though at a fairly low key; half a ship and some herring nets were purchased in the 1390s and there was further investment in the early 1400s. The boats owned by the monks in the fifteenth century involved little financial outlay, and were probably just rowing dinghies; but it is safe to assume that islanders also fished on their own behalf. Fish-processing continued in the priory precinct throughout the Middle Ages, and a fish house is among the buildings listed at the Reformation.

Fish tithes were paid to the monks at Tweed-mouth but also occasionally on Lindisfarne, and fluctuations in the value of the tithe indicate that there were fairly substantial variations in the supply of fish; cod and herring are the fish which feature most frequently. Archaeological finds from late-medieval deposits on the museum site contained the bones of cod, herring, whiting, haddock, eel and roker, and the size of fish caught supports the notion that the industry was organized and well developed. Both deep-water and inshore fishing were practised.

The documents also record the exploitation of the island quarries from the mid-fourteenth century, for both building stone and limeburning. The initial extraction seems to have been sparked by fairly extensive building works on the priory itself, but the last inventory of the priory includes some tools for limebreaking. None of the houses in the village are known to be of medieval origin, and it is possible that the medieval cottages were not built of stone. The priory accounts record the purchase of other building materials, such as iron, large structural timbers and straw for roofing. The use of 'bents' or coarse grass also features as a household consumable: this was possibly used for both flooring and thatch. Rabbits from the Snook were another source of revenue for the priory; the date of their introduction is not known but they first appear on parchment at

80 *The early stone revetment at the base of Jenny Bell's Well Midden.*

81 *Midden deposits at Jenny Bell's Well.*

the beginning of the fourteenth century. Tithes were collected on the warren; at a later stage the 'coneygarth' was leased.

The plan of the village deserves some comment. The island had a market charter in the later Middle Ages and this gave it a notional claim to town status. The basic elements of the plan must have been established in the medieval period: a mid-sixteenth century list of burgages on the island mentions properties on a number of the surviving streets. The Enclosure Award of 1791–2 is the earliest detailed scale map (**79**) and shows that by the end of the eighteenth century the plan was then similar in most respects to that of the present day. There are two open spaces: the market place, just north of the priory; and Fiddler's Green, to the west of this. The existence of two greens suggests that there may have been two different foci in the village in earlier times. The area to the west

of Fiddler's Green is now all pasture field, but excavations by Brian Hope-Taylor in the Vicar's Field, and our own work at Jenny Bell's Well Midden, indicate that the foreshore opposite St Cuthbert's Island was the centre of much greater activity in the past.

Underneath the midden a massive stone revetment was found, running parallel with the natural line of the cliff (**80**). This was overlain by the earliest midden deposits, which seemed to date from the thirteenth and fourteenth centuries (**81**). Investigations outside the excavation suggested that much of the area south of the revetment was made-up ground, with buildings underneath. Brian Hope-Taylor is also believed to have found thirteenth- and fourteenth-century buildings near this point, just back from the shore.

From the air (**82**) the remains of the long strips of open fields are clearly visible, extending nearly as far as Green Shiel, and these must reflect the pattern of cultivation at some point

82 *Aerial photograph showing ridge and furrow under the Lindisfarne dunes* (RCHM).

in time. However, it is difficult to assess the relative importance of different types of farming on the island in this period. The priory documents make specific reference to pasture, and record that the income from tithe corn on the island in the later Middle Ages was small, both of which hint that most of the land was even then given over to pasture. There is an early fourteenth-century reference to an assart, or reclaiming of land from the waste, and the wording of the document suggests that it was near the Snook, but we do not know to what purpose it was put.

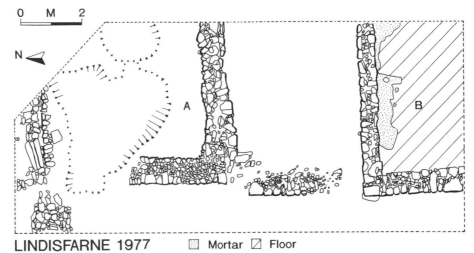

83 *Plan of early post-medieval buildings excavated on the site of the English Heritage museum.*

After the Dissolution

From the mid-sixteenth century, a rather clearer picture of the nature of the island community is possible. Parish records are intermittently available to provide a regular record of births, marriages and deaths; and the list of burgage plots referred to above indicates a fairly densely occupied village with a population probably no smaller than that of the present day.

Parts of two buildings of this period were excavated on the site of the new museum (**83**), and this provides some insight into standards of living at the time. The pottery from the excavation included a range of imported wares, from northern France, Germany and the Low Countries (**colour plate 14**) and there was even a small quantity of material of Spanish origin. The occurrence of this exotic material is not as surprising as it might at first seem; in this period many places along the eastern seaboard of Britain acquired imported pottery, often in substantial quantity, possibly because the native pottery industry was in decline or could not produce the attractive and fairly inexpensive wares available through the seaborne trade. The presence of the army garrison (however infrequently paid) would have helped to expand the market.

The two buildings on the museum site were fairly simple constructions, with clay-bonded walls of rough masonry, hinting that the priory was not yet available for despoliation. One had the remains of a mortared floor, and was presumably a dwelling-house; the other may have been an outbuilding or shed. These structures were abandoned towards the end of the seventeenth century, and the plot was left as an open space.

The animal bone evidence suggests the increasing professionalization of fishing. Large cod and flat fish are well represented, but from 1550–1600 to the present day herring is not represented at all. This must be some indication of the importance of this fish export; it is known that herring was extensively fished off the North Sea coast at this time but very little if any was actually consumed locally.

The excavation also produced evidence of the exploitation of molluscs and crustaceans in the village area. Winkles, oysters, limpets and whelks occur in all phases of the site, but cockles only occur in the early modern levels. Mussels are found in profusion in the early post-medieval phase; they are probably under-represented due to the rapidity with which their shells deteriorate in the ground. Crabs likewise are only found in the more recent deposits. All of the molluscs could have been used either as bait in line fishing or for food.

Much of the midden deposit at Jenny Bell's

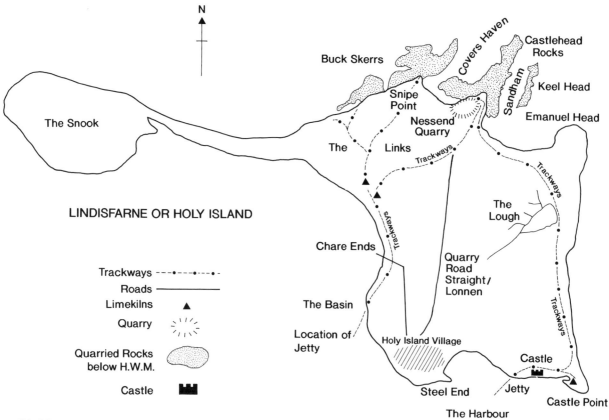

N

Buck Skerrs

Covers Haven

Castlehead Rocks

Snipe Point

Keel Head

The Snook

Nessend Quarry

Emanuel Head

Sandham

The   Links

Trackways

LINDISFARNE OR HOLY ISLAND

The Lough

Chare Ends

Trackways

Trackways

Quarry Road Straight/ Lonnen

Trackways	- - - ● - - ● -
Roads	————
Limekilns	▲
Quarry	☀
Quarried Rocks below H.W.M.	⬭
Castle	⬛

The Basin

Location of Jetty

Holy Island Village

Castle

Steel End

Jetty

Castle Point

The Harbour

84 *Map of industrial monuments on Lindisfarne* (after R. C. Jermy).

Well was of post-medieval date; in the seventeenth century the cliff edge was protected by a fence over which the villagers dumped quantities of shell and fish-bone. Certainly, by the seventeenth century, the fishing off Lindisfarne was good; there were about ninety individual householders on the island, many of whom were involved in this industry.

The eighteenth and nineteenth centuries
A wonderful bird's eye view of the island towards the beginning of the eighteenth century is provided by a document dating to 1721, first published anonymously by Raine:

> The town of Holy Island is an ancient town, and the inhabitants are distinguished into burgesses as they are called in ancient writings, or freemen, and stallengers. The burgesses or freemen are those who have houses in the town called freehold houses in number 24. The stallengers are those who are owners of the other houses. There are belonging to the freehold houses certain lands inclosed, as there are crofts and gardens belonging to the stallengers' houses. The rest of the island (save the lord's pasture) is a sandy soil whereon grows a sort of grass called bents, and is common among the freemen, who have a right to depasture a certain number of cattle thereon, and to cut the bents for covering their houses, to dig in the freestone quarries for stones for their use, to keep a fishing boat for the catching of codd and other fish, to cure and dry them on the common field, where there is a place made for the purpose, and to draw their boats for safety above the full sea mark, and lay them there on the said common. Only they pay tithes to the Lord of the Mannor. The

stallengers have a right to depasture their cattle there also, but they are stinted to a lesser number than the freemen are.

The Enclosure Act of 1791, seventy years later, suggests that there was little change in agricultural practice in the intervening period; the infield consisted of only *c.* 20–25 acres. The accompanying map (see **79**) indicates that most of the island was open common, used for grazing. The act also shows the island poised on the brink of industrial development, as authority was given to erect a kiln for lime burning for 'the general benefit'.

There is abundant archaeological evidence of the limestone extraction and limeburning industry on Lindisfarne which developed in the course of the nineteenth century (**84**). The island was covered in a series of tracks and waggonways linking the outcrops on the north coast with a number of kilns, and jetties were constructed by the castle and Tripping Chare to offload the cargo.

There are two main groups of limekilns on Lindisfarne. On the border between the dunes and the north-west extent of modern farmland are the ruins of the Kennedy Limeworks, now totally overgrown and covered by sand. This was an extensive complex. Two partly collapsed bottle kilns are visible today facing the track at the northern edge of the site. These were built by a local partnership, Messrs Gibson and Lumsden of Belford, and were in use for a short period in the 1840s. The waggonway which partly destroyed the site at Green Shiel was constructed to transport limestone from the quarries at Nessend and Snipe Point to this site for processing, and then onwards to a stone and timber jetty south of Chare Ends, from where it was shipped along the coast. In the late 1850s these kilns were replaced by a group of three to the south. The new kilns were built 'in error' by one William Nicholl, a lime merchant of Dundee who leased the extraction rights from Donaldson Selby, and were only in use for a couple of years, Nicholl relocating

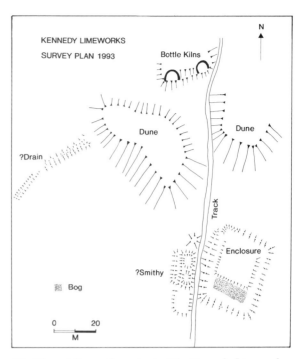

85 *Plan of the northern part of the Kennedy Limeworks, showing bottle kilns, the smithy and an enclosure.*

his enterprise in 1860. These short-lived kilns survive as a rectangular shell at the terminus of the large waggonway embankment encircling the area of modern farmland.

Between the two kiln groups are a number of buildings which served the limeworks (**85**). The low earthworks of a small cottage to the south of the bottle kilns are recorded as a smithy on the first Ordnance Survey map. Facing this on the other side of the track is a rectangular enclosure with an entrance in its north-west corner; both of these features overlie the ridge-and-furrow ploughing in this area. South-east of these is a row of walled, open bays; these were recorded as limekilns on the first Ordnance map but they are much more likely to have been used for stables or storage (**86**). Another ruined and overgrown site lies at the northern end of the raised waggonway: this seems to consist of two buildings and a stone-lined well inside a walled enclosure (**87**).

The best-preserved limeworks are those at Castle Point, which are now in the care of the

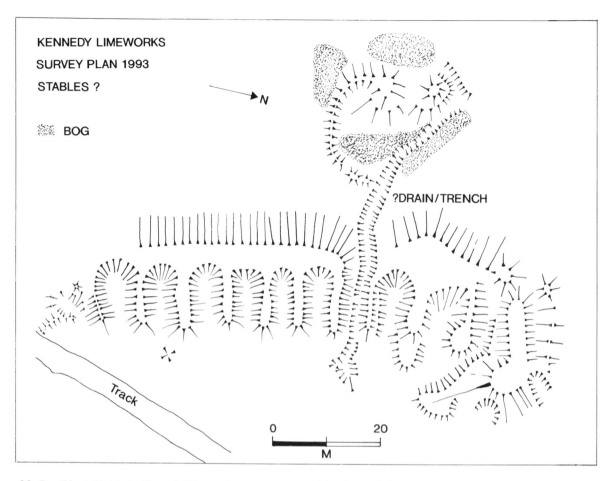

KENNEDY LIMEWORKS
SURVEY PLAN 1993
STABLES ?

▒ BOG

→N

?DRAIN/TRENCH

Track

0   20
M

86 *Possible stable block, Kennedy Limeworks.*

National Trust (**88**). These were constructed by William Nicholl as a replacement for the kilns at the Kennedy site, and were in use for about twenty years. Their development involved the construction of a further tramway along the east coast, still a conspicuous feature of the island landscape, and another pier to the south-west of the castle, the remains of which can still be seen at low tide. Nicholl shipped his product from here to Dundee in a number of different vessels, which returned with coal to fuel the kilns.

In their restored state the castle kilns are an impressive monument to the scale of industrial enterprise on Lindisfarne in the nineteenth century, but this was a fairly short-lived boom. There are six separate pots in a rectangular

block, and they seem to have processed about 3000 tons of stone per annum in their heyday. Nicholl's lease specified that he should extract no more than 5000 tons in any one year, so he was clearly not working at full capacity. By the early 1880s limeburning had become a highly seasonal activity and seems to have totally ceased by 1885. The kilns were apparently last fired about 1900.

There were a number of other industrial initiatives on Lindisfarne in the eighteenth and nineteenth centuries, which either failed to get off the ground or were very short-lived. There are records of ironstone being extracted in the late eighteenth century from outcrops below the high-tide mark, but plans to revive this in the mid-nineteenth century came to nothing. A project to set up a brick and tile works using the local clay was reported in the *Berwick*

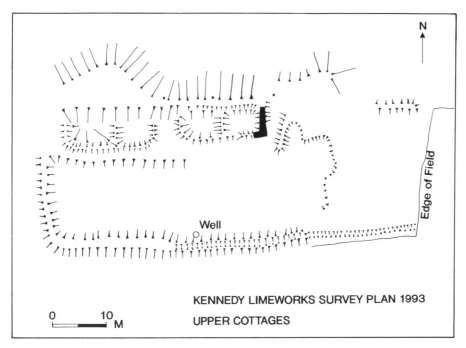

KENNEDY LIMEWORKS SURVEY PLAN 1993

UPPER COTTAGES

Well

Edge of Field

N

0   10 M

87 *The ruined cottages north-east of the Kennedy Limeworks.*

88 *The limekilns by the castle.*

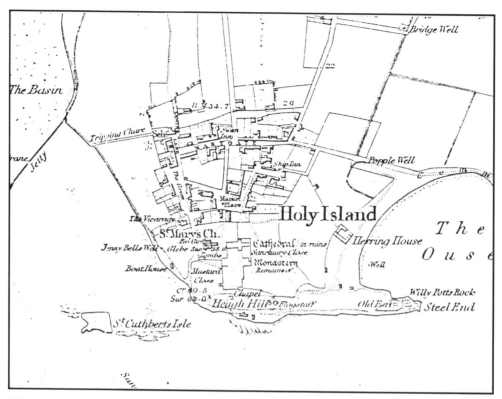

89 *The village, as shown on the first edition of the Ordnance Survey map* (Crown copyright).

Advertiser in 1846; there is no sign that this scheme was ever implemented, however.

Attempts to mine coal on the island are better attested: coal pits were apparently in operation at the end of the Snook in the 1790s, and there is also a record of workings further east, possibly near Green Shiel at this time. In the 1840s Donaldson Selby tried to develop more extensive workings near Snook House. The tower which can still be seen on the Snook covers the top of a disused shaft.

The mid-nineteenth century census material and the first Ordnance Survey map indicate a fairly large population (**89**) and one growing more rapidly than that of the mainland chapelries of Holy Island parish, as the table shows:

Year	Island	Mainland chapelries	Total parish population
1841	497	310	807
1851	553	307	860
1861	614	318	932

Population of Holy Island Parish 1841–61

The importance of fishing in the island's economy fluctuated dramatically in the eighteenth and nineteenth centuries. A decline is noted in the early 1700s, and seems to have continued until the turn of the century, when there was an upswing, due to the growing success of the herring fisheries. This reached an all-time peak in the mid-nineteenth century, when it is estimated that about 50 per cent of the population was involved in the industry. By the time of the First World War herring fishing was, in turn, of no consequence on the island. Declining herring stocks, motorized drifters and the nature of the harbour all conspired to bring the herring boom to a close, although line fishing, and the catching of lobsters and crabs remained important. The importance of salmon, taken with static nets off the North Shore of the island also increased in the nineteenth century.

The three-storeyed Herring Houses on the shore by the harbour (**90**) are visible evidence of the fish-curing which was customary on this

90 *The Herring Houses.*

part of the common and which is referred to in the 1721 document cited above. In the nineteenth century it was here that the herring were cleaned and smoked before packing and export. Other structures in the village, now converted into dwellings, also functioned as smoke houses. The upturned boats on the shore by the harbour and on the Castle Rock are also mute evidence of the once thriving herring industry. These are the remains of the large sail-powered boats of the late nineteenth century which harvested this rich resource, and now function as sheds and lock-ups for the modern fishermen's equipment (**91**).

The island community today
Lindisfarne has been the subject of two recent population studies, one in 1969 when Dr. R. A. Cartwright carried out the research for his 1973, Ph.D. thesis, *Holy Island, a Demographic, Genetical and Medical Population Study*, and one done as part of our own research on Lindisfarne in April 1990 and April 1992. The adult population now stands at about 190, an increase of 15 since Cartwright's study but a substantial decrease since the mid-nineteenth century.

Increasingly, islanders have fewer kin ties – the majority of the present population were not born on the island and are not closely related to those who were. Despite this, the islander's sense of identity remains buoyant, and many local customs and practices continue to thrive.

The recent decline of fishing has been quite dramatic: in 1992, there were only 15 people for whom fishing was the sole occupation,

91 *Holy Island (c. 1950s) before recent development* (Cambridge University, Air Photo Library).

distributed among 7 boats. Inshore crabs and lobsters were the main harvest; mussels are also still collected, from beds which have been established in Budle Bay and off Guile Point, but the beds close to the island are frequently now contaminated by red algae, which renders them potentially dangerous for human consumption.

The island's historic past is today the main source of its income: tourism is now the most significant industry, and the majority of the island's population are involved in it in some form, either through the provision of food, accommodation or other services, or directly employed by English Heritage or the National Trust. Visitors are not only welcome, but important to the well-being of the island economy.

Lindisfarne Castle and Lindisfarne Priory are among the most popular of historic sites in northern England, but very few of the hundreds of thousands of their visitors wander far from the well-beaten path between the village and the Castle Rock. For many reasons this is perhaps fortunate: the special character of the island's natural attractions and the bright open landscape are best appreciated in tranquillity, and the solitary wanderer offers little threat to the well-being of the Nature Reserve.

Absorbing the seeming harmony between natural surroundings, sites, fields and settlement, many might be tempted to view Lindisfarne as fixed in time. The impression of an unchanging past is always an illusion, however, and this is particularly true of this small island, with its unusually ambiguous and liminal relationship to the mainland. Even today it is still capable of transformation by wholly natural processes, and much of its recent history now lies covered by the dunes.

What to see on and around Lindisfarne

The list of sites, monuments and museums which follows is a personal choice on the part of the authors. Opening times and admission prices were correct at the time of writing, but may be subject to change; it would be advisable always to check.

On Lindisfarne

English Heritage Properties

Lindisfarne Priory. Opening times: 1 Apr–30 Sept; open daily 10am–6pm. 1 Oct–31 Mar; open Tue–Sun 10am–4pm. Adults £2.00, concessions £1.50, children £1.00. English Heritage members free. Special party rates. Admission includes access to site museum. Opening times are subject to tides; check tide tables before setting out. Tel. 0289 89200.

National Trust Properties

Lindisfarne Castle. Opening times: Apr–Oct; open daily 1pm–5pm except Fridays. Adults £3.40, children £1.70. No concessions or party rates. National Trust members free. Tel. 0289 89244.

The Parish Church of St Mary is also an important architectural feature on the island. It is largely thirteenth century in date but contains fragments of earlier masonry.

Around Lindisfarne

The countryside around the island is a marvellous place to visit. Northumberland County Council's Tourist Office can provide detailed leaflets for the whole county and can be contacted via The Tourism Office, Northumberland Business Centre, Southgate, Morpeth, NE61 2EH. Tel. 0670 533924. Tourist Information Centres are located in the following towns close to Lindisfarne. Telephone numbers are included. Alnwick 0665 510665; Berwick 0289 330733; Hexham 0434 605225; Morpeth 0670 511323; Blyth Valley Public Relations Office 0670 355521; Wansbeck Leisure and Publicity Dept. Ashington 0670 814444.

English Heritage Properties

1 Berwick-upon-Tweed Barracks Museum. Opening times: 1 Apr–30 Sept; open daily 10am–6pm. 1 Oct–31 Mar; open Tue–Sun 10am–4pm. Adults £2.00, concessions £1.50, children £1.00. English Heritage members free. Special party rates. An award-winning museum well worth seeing.

2 Berwick-upon-Tweed Ramparts. Elizabethan fortifications. Free admission at any reasonable time.

Also worth a visit is the Borough Museum and Art Gallery in the Clock Block of the Barracks. This houses material from the famous Burrell Collection. Open as Barracks. For details Tel. 0289 304493. The Museum of the King's Own Scottish Borderers is also located within the Barracks.

3 Dunstanburgh Castle. Opening times: 1 Apr–30 Sept; open daily 10am–6pm. 1 Oct–31 Mar; open Tue–Sun 10am–4pm. Adults £1.20,

concessions 90p, children 60p. English Heritage members free. Special party rates. Located 8 miles NE of Alnwick, reached by footpath either N from Craster (1½ miles) or S from Embleton (2 miles). Tel. 0665 576231.

4 Brinkburn Priory. Opening times: 1 Apr–30 Sept; open daily 10am–6pm. Adults £1.20, concessions 90p, children 60p. English Heritage members free. Special party rates. 4½ miles SE of Rothbury off B6334. Tel. 0665 570628.

5 Warkworth Castle. Opening times: 1 Apr–30 Sept; open daily 10am–6pm. 1 Oct–31 Mar; open Tue–Sun 10am–4pm. Adults £1.70, concessions £1.30, children 85p. English Heritage members free. Special party rates. Located in Warkworth, 7½ miles S of Alnwick on A1068. Tel. 0665 711423.

6 Norham Castle. Opening times: 1 Apr–30 Sept; open daily 10am–6pm. 1 Oct–31 Mar; open Tue–Sun 10am–4pm. At the time of writing no full-time warden was available at the site. Located in Norham Village. Tel. 0289 382329.

7 Edlingham Castle. Open any reasonable time. Free admission. This castle is well worth a visit. SE of Alnwick off B6341. Edlingham church is also an under-visited treasure.

Other non-English Heritage properties in the area include, Bamburgh Castle, Chillingham Castle, famous for its herd of wild cattle, Cragside House, Wallington Hall and Seaton Delaval Hall. Hadrian's Wall is also within striking distance of Lindisfarne as is the beautiful unspoilt countryside of the Cheviot Hills.

Further reading

General Works

There are a couple of modern general books about Lindisfarne which partly deal with its archaeology and history: R. A. Cartwright and D. B. Cartwright (1976), *The Holy Island of Lindisfarne and the Farne Islands* (Newton Abbot: David and Charles) and M. Magnusson (1984), *Lindisfarne, The Cradle Island* (Stocksfield: Oriel Press). J. Raine (1852), *The History and Antiquities of North Durham* (Durham: G. Andrews) publishes much helpful primary source material. W. Hutchinson (1785–94), *The History and Antiquities of the County Palatine of Durham* (Newcastle: S. Hodgson) is also useful, and fairly widely available.

Archaeological work on the island

There are a number of published accounts of early visits by antiquarians and naturalists to the island including G. Johnston, 'Our visit to Holy Island in May, 1854' *History of the Berwickshire Naturalist's Club*, 7 (1873–5), 27–52; and Anon 'Holy Island' *Proceedings of the Society of Antiquaries of Newcastle upon Tyne*, 3rd Ser. Vol. III (1908), 285–311.

Crossman's work is published in W. Crossman, 'The recent excavations at Holy Island Priory' *History of the Berwickshire Naturalist's Club*, 13 (1892), 225–40 and 'Chapel of St Cuthbert-in-the-Sea' *History of the Berwickshire Naturalist's Club*, 13 (1892), 241–2. The discovery of the hearth sites is reported by W. de L. Aitcheson in *Proceedings of the Society of Antiquaries of Newcastle upon Tyne*, 4th Ser. (1937–8), 116–18. The excavations on the site of the museum are described in D. M. O'Sullivan *et al.*, 'An excavation in Holy Island village, 1977' *Archaeologia Aeliana*, 5th Ser. 13 (1985), 27–116.

A number of interim publications arising from the Lindisfarne Research Project by P. Beavitt, D. O'Sullivan and R. Young have appeared: (1985), *Recent Fieldwork on Lindisfarne* (University of Leicester, Department of Archaeology Occasional Paper No 1); (1986), *Holy Island: a Guide to Current Archaeological Research* (University of Leicester: Department of Archaeology); 'Fieldwork on Lindisfarne, Northumberland, 1980–1988' *Northern Archaeology*, 8 (1987), 1–23 and (1988), *Archaeology on Lindisfarne* (University of Leicester: Department of Archaeology).

The changing environment of Lindisfarne

There are a few books available dealing with the geology of north-east England, one of the more recent being D. A. Robson (1980), *The Geology of North-East England* (Newcastle upon Tyne: The Natural History Society of Northumbria). For specific information on the geology and geomorphology of Lindisfarne itself the following small publications have been produced: D. A. Robson (1982), *The Geology of Holy Island* (Newcastle, Nature Conservancy Council) and J. A. Galliers (1970),

The Geomorphology of Holy Island (University of Newcastle upon Tyne: Department of Geography Research Series No. 6).

For those with an interest in natural history there are plenty of excellent field guides available, the best usually those published by Collins (London). These include *The Collins Pocket Guide to the Sea Shore* by J. Barrett and C. M. Yonge (1958), *The Collins Guide to the Grasses, Sedges, Rushes and Ferns of Britain and Northern Europe* by R. Fitter (1984), and by the same author, *The Collins New Generation Guide: Wild Flowers of Britain and Northern Europe* (1987). In the same 'New Generation' series is the guide by C. Perrin (1987), *Birds of Britain and Northern Europe.* For those with a real interest, there are some more extensive guides to the flora of Britain; a beautifully illustrated and 'user-friendly' guide is M. Blamey and C. Grey-Wilson (1989), *The Illustrated Flora of Britain and Northern Europe* (London: Hodder and Stoughton). For the keen and more experienced botanist the definitive volume is C. Stace (1991), *New Flora of the British Isles* (Cambridge: University Press). Two short pamphlets deal with bird-life of the Lindisfarne area: P. Hawkey (1990), *Birds of the Farnes* (Rothbury: Butler Publishing) and I. Kerr (1992), *Lindisfarne's Birds* (Morpeth: Northumberland and Tyneside Bird Club).

Prehistory on Lindisfarne
Stray finds of prehistoric material on Lindisfarne are reported in F. Buckley, 'Some flints of the Tardenois period from Scrog Hill, Dunstanburgh, Holy Island and Craster, Northumberland' *Proceedings of the Society of Antiquaries of Newcastle upon Tyne*, 4th Ser. 1 (1935–6), 42–7 and R. Coleman-Smith, 'A bronze-age spearhead from Holy Island' *Archaeologia Aeliana*, 5th Ser. 7 (1979), 245–6. Preliminary accounts of our work at Nessend appear in the general papers by Beavitt, O'Sullivan and Young cited above.

Early work on the northern coastal Mesolithic is described in F. Buckley, 'The microlithic industries of Northumberland' *Archaeologia*

Aeliana, 4th Ser. 1 (1925), 42–7; A. Raistrick, 'Mesolithic sites on the northeast coast of England' *Proceedings of the Prehistoric Society of East Anglia*, 7 (1933) 188–98; A. Raistrick, 'The distribution of Mesolithic sites in the north of England' *Yorkshire Archaeological Journal*, 31 (1933), 141–56; C. T. Trechmann, 'Neolithic remains on the Durham Coast' *The Naturalist*, 587 (1905), 361–3; C. T. Trechmann, 'Mesolithic flints from the submerged forest at West Hartlepool' *Proceedings of the Prehistoric Society*, 2 (1936), 161–8; and C.T. Trechmann, 'The submerged forest beds of the Durham coast' *Proceedings of the Yorkshire Geological Society*, 27 (i) (1946), 23–32.

The natural sources of lithic material in the north are considered by C. Wickham Jones and G. Collins, 'The sources of flint and chert in northern Britain' *Proceedings of the Society of Antiquaries of Scotland*, 109 (1977–8), 7–21; and R. Young, 'Potential sources of flint and chert in the north-east of England' *Lithics*, 5 (1984), 3–9.

The Anglo-Saxon monastery
The early history of Northumbria is extensively covered in standard works, such as those of P. Hunter Blair (1976), *Northumbria in the Days of Bede* (London: Gollancz); P. Hunter Blair (1970), *The World of Bede* (London: Secker and Warburg) and H. Mayr-Harting (1972), *The Coming of Christianity to Anglo-Saxon England* (London: Batsford). N. Higham (1992), *The Kingdom of Northumbria AD 350–1100* (Stroud: Alan Sutton Publishing); B. Yorke (1990), *Kings and Kingdoms in Early Anglo-Saxon England* (London: Seaby); D. P. Kirby (1991), *The Earliest English Kings* (London: Unwin Hyman) and D. Dumville (1989), 'The origins of Northumbria: some aspects of the British background' in S. Bassett (ed.), *The Origins of Anglo-Saxon Kingdoms* (Leicester: University Press), 213–22 are more recent evaluations. B. Hope-Taylor (1977), *Yeavering: An Anglo-British centre of early Northumbria*, Department of the Environment Archaeological Report No. 7

(London: HMSO) provides a more archaeologically oriented approach.

The original account of the Battle of Lindisfarne is critically considered by D. Dumville, 'On the North British section of the *Historia Brittonum' Welsh History Review*, 8 (1976–7), 345–54. It is also discussed in I. Lovecy, 'The end of Celtic Britain: a sixth-century battle near Lindisfarne' *Archaeologia Aeliana*, 5th Ser. 4 (1976), 31–45.

R. Cramp, 'Anglo-Saxon Monasteries of the North' *Scottish Archaeological Forum*, 5 (1973), 104–24; R. Cramp (1976), 'Monastic sites' in D.M. Wilson (ed.), *The Archaeology of Anglo-Saxon England* (London: Methuen); and R. Cramp (1984), *The Hermitage and the Offshore Island* (London: National Maritime Museum Occasional Lecture No. 3) provide general accounts of early Northumbrian monasticism. B. Colgrave and R. A. B. Mynors (ed. and trans. 1969), *Bede's Ecclesiastical History of the English People* (Oxford: Clarendon Press) and A. Campbell (ed. and trans. 1967), *De Abbatibus* (Oxford: University Press) are important primary sources.

The best account of the physical remains on Iona is contained in The Royal Commission on the Ancient and Historical Monuments of Scotland (1982), *Argyll: An Inventory of the Monuments. Vol. 4: Iona* (Edinburgh: HMSO). A.D.S. MacDonald, 'Aspects of the monastery and monastic life in Adamnan's Life of St Columba' *Peritia*, 3 (1984), 271–302 discusses the documentary evidence for the monastic buildings. C. Thomas (1971), *The Early Christian Archaeology of North Britain* (Oxford: University Press) is still useful as a general background.

There are a number of papers which consider the monastery on Lindisfarne itself in Bonner *et al.* (see section on St Cuthbert below), especially D. O'Sullivan, 'The plan of the early Christian monastery on Lindisfarne: a fresh look at the evidence' 125–42. J. Blair, 'The early churches at Lindisfarne' *Archaeologia Aeliana*, 5th Ser. 19 (1991), 47–54 discusses the alignment of the later medieval churches.

The landholdings of the Lindisfarne community are discussed in C. D. Morris, 'Northumbria and the Viking settlement: the evidence of landholding' *Archaeologia Aeliana*, 5th Ser. 5 (1977), 81–103; E. Craster, 'The patrimony of St Cuthbert' *English Historical Review*, 69 (1954), 177–99; and G. Jones, 'Historical Geography and our landed heritage' *University of Leeds Review*, 19 (1976), 53–78. P.H. Sawyer (1978), 'Sources for the History of Viking Northumbria' in R.A. Hall (ed.), *Viking Age York and the North* (London: Council for British Archaeology Research Report 27) 3–7 briefly considers the monastery in the ninth century.

There is no modern edition for the important later sources, *Historia de Sancto Cuthberto* and *Historia Dunelmensis Ecclesiae*, but there are two Victorian editions, T. Arnold (ed. 1882), *Symeonis Monachi Opera Omnia* (London: Rolls series Vol 1) and J. Hodgson Hinde (1868), *Symeonis Dunelmensis Opera et Collectanea* (Durham: Surtees Society Vol. 51).

The Anglo-Saxon carvings on the island were first drawn to scholarly attention in J. Stuart (ed. 1856–67), *Sculptured Stones of Scotland* 2 vols, (Aberdeen: Spalding Club). The Lindisfarne stones are considered in Vol. II, 19–20, pl XXVI. Most of those found subsequently are dealt with in C.R. Peers, 'The inscribed and sculptured stones of Lindisfarne' *Archaeologia*, 74 (1925), 255–70, but the standard work of reference for the Anglo-Saxon sculpture is now R. Cramp (1984), *Corpus of Anglo-Saxon Stone Sculpture in England, Vol. I. Northumberland and Durham* (Oxford: University Press) 194–208, which deals specifically with the Lindisfarne carvings.

St Cuthbert and Lindisfarne

B. Colgrave (ed. and trans. 1940; reprinted 1985), *Two lives of St Cuthbert* (Cambridge: University Press) contains the most important primary sources. G. Bonner, D.W. Rollason and C. Stanncliffe (eds 1989), *St Cuthbert, his Cult and his Community to AD 1200* (Woodbridge: Boydell Press) is an important collection of papers on all aspects of St Cuthbert and his cult, and D.W. Rollason (ed. 1987), *Cuthbert: Saint and Patron* (Durham: Cathedral Dean and Chapter) is also useful. M. Baker, 'Medieval illustrations of Bede's Life of Cuthbert' *Journal of the Warburg and Courtauld Institutes*, 41 (1978), 16–49 extends the study of St Cuthbert's cult into the high Middle Ages.

The Lindisfarne Gospels are fully discussed in the facsimile edition: T.D. Kendrick *et al.* (eds 1956–60), *Evangeliorum quattuor Codex Lindisfarnensis, Musei Britannici Codex Cottonianus Nero D.IV* 2 vols (Lausanne: Urs Graf Verlag). There is a facsimile edition of the Durham Gospels: C. Verey, T.J. Brown and E. Coastworth (ed.s 1980), *The Durham Gospels* (Copenhagen: Early English Manuscripts in Facsimile 20). Good introductions to Insular manuscript art are now available including G. Henderson (1987), *From Durrow to Kells: the insular gospel books 650–800* (London: Thames and Hudson); J. Alexander (1978), *Insular Manuscripts, Sixth to Ninth Century* (London: Harvey Miller); and C. Nordenfalk (1977), *Celtic and Anglo-Saxon Painting: book illumination in the British Isles 600–800* (London: Chatto and Windus). J. Backhouse (1981), *The Lindisfarne Gospels* (Oxford: Phaidon) is an easily available consideration of this manuscript and there are several discussions of the work of the Lindisfarne scriptorium in the proceedings of the 1987 Cuthbert conference (Bonner *et al.*, cited above).

The original account of the 1827 discovery of St Cuthbert's relics is found in J. Raine (1828), *St Cuthbert, with an account of the state in which his remains were found upon the opening of his tomb in Durham Cathedral, in the year 1827* (Durham: G. Andrews).

The definitive publication of the relics is that of C. F. Battiscombe (ed. 1956), *The Relics of St Cuthbert* (Oxford: University Press). Bonner *et al.* (cited above) contains some important revisions of this material. Recent work on the coffin is published in J. M. Cronyn and C. V. Horie (1985), *St Cuthbert's Coffin: the history, technology and conservation* (Durham: Cathedral Dean and Chapter).

The medieval priory

Lindisfarne Priory is described or discussed in a number of general studies of medieval monasticism, including L. Butler and C. Given-Wilson, *Medieval Monasteries of Great Britain* (London: Michael Joseph) 283–6 and D. Knowles and J.K. St Joseph (1952), *Monastic Sites from the Air* (Cambridge: University Press) 40–1. The most extensive account of the history of the medieval priory is contained in Raine (1852), cited above. E. Cambridge (1988), *Lindisfarne Priory and Holy Island* (London: English Heritage) is a short general guide.

A.H. Thompson (1949), *Lindisfarne Priory, Northumberland* (London: HMSO) and J.P. McAleer, 'The upper nave elevation and high vaults of Lindisfarne Priory' *Durham Archaeological Journal*, 2 (1986), 43–53 discuss the architectural history of the monument.

Green Shiel

The original discovery of the site at Green Shiel is noted in J.S.D. Selby, 'On the Foundations of Ancient Buildings, and Coins of the Saxon Kingdom of Northumbria, recently discovered at Holy Island' *History of the Berwickshire Naturalist's Club*, 11 (1849), 159–63. In addition to general accounts of our recent research, the excavations at Green Shiel have been specifically dealt with in two articles: D. O'Sullivan and R. Young, 'The early medieval settlement at Green Shiel, Northumberland' *Archaeologia Aeliana*, 5th Ser. 19 (1991), 55–70, and D. O'Sullivan and R. Young, 'The early medieval settlement at Green Shiel, Lindisfarne. An interim report on the excavations, 1984–91' *Archaeology North*, 2 (1991), 17–21.

Contemporary early medieval settlements in the north are published in D. Coggins, K. Fairless and C. E. Batey, 'Simy Folds: an early medieval settlement in Upper Teesdale' *Medieval Archaeology*, 27 (1983), 1–26; A. King (1978), 'Gauber High Pasture, Ribblehead – an interim report' in R. A. Hall, (ed.), *Viking Age York and the North* (London: Council for British Archaeology Research Report 27) 21–5 and

S. Dickinson (1985), 'Bryant's Gill, Kentmere: another "Viking-Period" Ribblehead?' in J. R. Baldwin and R.D. Whyte (eds), *The Scandinavians in Cumbria* (Edinburgh: Scottish Society for Northern Research).

Secular Anglo-Saxon building traditions in the north-east are discussed in S. James, A. Marshall and M. Millett, 'An early medieval building tradition' *Archaeological Journal*, 141 (1984), 182–215; T. Gates and C. O'Brien, 'Crop marks at Milfield and New Bewick and the recognition of Grübenhauser in Northumberland' *Archaeologia Aeliana*, 5th Ser. 16 (1988), 1–9; C. O'Brien and R. Miket, 'The early medieval settlement of Thirlings, Northumberland' *Durham Archaeological Journal*, 7 (1991), 57–91; see also B. Hope-Taylor (1978), *Yeavering* cited above.

The island fortifications
The most important discussion of the fortification of Holy Island is contained in M. Merriman and J. Summerson (1982), 'The Scottish Border' in H.M. Colvin (ed.), *The History of the Kings Works* (London: HMSO) 607–728. Also, see A.J. Lilburn, 'Seventeenth-century accounts relating to forts on Holy Island and at the mouth of the Tyne, 1675 to 1681' *Archaeologia Aeliana*, 5th Ser. 14 (1986), 135–43.

G. Bruce, 'The English expedition into Scotland in 1542' *Archaeologia Aeliana*, 3rd Ser. 3 (1907), 191–212 describes the circumstances which surrounded the fortification of Lindisfarne. The text of Sir Robert Bowes' Border Survey is published in J. Hodgson (1813), *A History of Northumberland* part 3, Vol II, 171–248 (London: Sherwood, Nealy and Jones).

P. Anderson Graham, 'Lindisfarne Castle, Northumberland: a residence of Mr Edward Hudson' *Country Life*, 33 (1913), 830–42; C. Amery (1982), *Lindisfarne Castle, an illustrated souvenir* (London: National Trust) and P. Orde (n.d.), *Lindisfarne Castle* (London: National Trust; attrib. various authors in later editions to 1986) describe the castle in its restored form.

The island community
Lindisfarne parish church has been briefly described in a number of works on church architecture; see especially F.R. Wilson (1870), *An architectural survey of the churches in the archdeaconry of Lindisfarne* (Newcastle: M. and M. W. Lambert) 18–20; N. Pevsner (1957), *The Buildings of England: Northumberland* (Harmondsworth: Penguin) 188; H. M. and J. Taylor (1965–78), *Anglo-Saxon Architecture* (Cambridge: University Press) 398–9 and R. Bailey, E. Cambridge and H. D. Briggs (1988), *Dowsing in Church Archaeology* (Wimborne: Intercept) 83–5.

Much of the published information about the recent history of the island is contained in general works. The population history of the island to *c.* 1971 has been considered in detail by R. A. Cartwright (1973), 'The Structure of populations living on Holy Island, Northumberland' in D. F. Roberts and E. Sunderland (ed.s), *Genetic Variation in Britain*, Symposia of the Society for the Study of Human Biology, Vol. 12 (London: Taylor and Francis) 95–108. See also R. A. Cartwright (1973), *Holy Island, A Demographic, Genetic and Medical Population Study*, Ph.D. Thesis, University of Durham. R. C. Jermy (1992), *Lindisfarne's Limestone Past: quarries, tramways and kilns* (Morpeth: Northumberland County Library) describes industrial monuments on the island.

Glossary

In compiling this glossary we have drawn upon the following sources: *Oxford English Dictionary*; S. Champion, 1980, *A Dictionary of Terms and Techniques in Archaeology*, Phaidon Press, Oxford; P. Bahn (ed.), 1992, *Collins Dictionary of Archaeology*, Harper Collins, London; and F.H. Goodyear, 1971, *Archaeological Site Science*, Heinemann, London.

aumbry A cupboard, locker or closed recess in a wall for books, sacramental vessels and vestments etc. in a church.

barbed-and-tanged arrowhead An arrowhead form, usually of Bronze Age date in Britain, made on a flint flake or blade. Usually roughly triangular in shape, the base of the triangle being worked with two notches to form a central tang for attaching the head to a shaft. The two symmetrical barbs at either side of the tang, caused by the notching, give it its other characteristic features.

BP Literally 'before present'. A convention adopted in the presentation of radiocarbon dates. For this purpose, 'the present' begins in 1950.

Bronze Age The period of antiquity in the Old World when bronze became a primary material for weapons and tools. In Europe there are three basic phases; early, middle and late, conventionally spanning the period *c.* 2000BC–700BC.

burgage A tenure whereby lands or tenements in cities and towns were held of the king or other lord for certain yearly rents. The term also applies to freehold properties in a borough. The area rented is sometimes referred to as a 'burgage plot' and is often delimited by walls.

chancel The eastern part of a church in which the clergy officiate. It usually contains the altar or communion table and is often separated from the main body of the church, the nave, by a rail or screen.

digital terrain model A detailed contour-based model or map of a piece of landscape, usually generated using an electronic distance measurer (see below) which can be digitized for computer manipulation to produce a three-dimensional representation of the area which is then capable of being viewed from different perspectives and at different scales.

echelon A geological formation.

electronic distance measurer A surveying instrument which utilizes laser light and a complex arrangement of prisms to measure distances, angles and heights, automatically, without recourse to standard tape and other measurement techniques.

geophysical survey A method of surveying designed to locate archaeological features without digging. Such methods use instruments that measure the physical properties of surface materials. The main method used on Lindisfarne has been resistivity surveying, in which an electrical current is passed through the soil between electrodes and the resistance of the soil to that current is recorded. A low resistance is due to increased soil moisture and may indicate the presence of cut features such as pits and ditches. A high resistance is due to a decrease in soil moisture and may be caused by the presence of buried features such as walls.

grübenhaus A German term for a structure with a dug-out or sunken floor, usually of Anglo-Saxon date. Sometimes referred to as 'sunken featured' buildings. There is some debate as to whether such structures are actual dwellings or ancillary/workshop-type buildings on settlement sites.

leaf-shaped arrowhead A projectile point, usually of Neolithic date, made on a flint flake or blade. Characterized by a roughly oval, leaf-like shape, hence the name, and usually worked on both faces by either pressure flaking or by controlled direct percussion. Sometimes referred to as 'foliate' forms.

lithic scatter A surface scatter of humanly struck stone material. Usually these comprise the finished tools, the debris from stone working and chunks of the raw material used in initial artefact preparation, in various proportions.

maniple An ecclesiastical vestment worn by a priest during the Eucharist service. Consists of a strip of cloth around 1m in length, worn hanging from the left arm. Said to have been originally a napkin.

Mesolithic Literally, 'middle stone age'. Traditionally the period of transition between the Palaeolithic (old stone age) and Neolithic (new stone age), which saw the continued development of complex hunting/gathering and fishing techniques, as climate ameliorated after the retreat of the glacial ice sheet around *c.* 8500BC.

microlith A small stone tool made on a blade or flake. Often these are smaller than 2cm in length and occur in geometric shapes. Traditionally seen as the armatures for composite arrowheads. It is a typical Mesolithic artefact type.

Neolithic (see Mesolithic above). Traditionally the period in the Old World when people began to farm and evolve sedentary settlement patterns, to use pottery and to use polished stone implements such as axes.

piscina A perforated stone basin, recessed into the wall of a church, usually on the south side of the altar.

quoining The stone- or brickwork forming the quoin or angle of a wall (can be either internal or external).

radiocarbon dating A technique for determining the age of carbon-bearing materials based on the known rate of decay of the radioactive isotope Carbon-14. All living organisms absorb a proportion of Carbon-14 during their lifetime, from the atmosphere and/or the food chain. Upon death this absorption stops and the process of radioactive decay begins. Determination of the radioactivity of carbon from a sample will reveal the proportion of Carbon-14 to the inert form of Carbon-12 and this in turn will, through the known rate of decay of Carbon-14, give the time that has elapsed since the death of the sample.

remanent magnetism The magnetism remaining in baked clay when it cools down after being heated in a magnetic field. In pottery and archaeological features with burnt clay such as hearths, it is assumed that the field was the earth's magnetic field and estimates of the direction and intensity of the latter may be made from measurements of thermo-remanent magnetism. The property is used in both dating and geophysical surveying.

resistivity surveying See geophysical survey.

scriptorium A room in a religious house used for the copying or writing of manuscripts.

shiel A small house or cottage, often only occupied for part of the year. Shiels or shielings, which were seasonally occupied by herders and shepherds are a common feature of the Northumberland and Borders uplands.

stole An ecclesiastical vestment consisting of a strip of silk or linen worn over a cleric's shoulders, hanging down in front or crossed over the breast.

styca A small bronze coin current in Northumbria in the eighth to ninth centuries AD.

tombolo Technically a bar, usually of sand or gravel, joining an island to the mainland. At certain times but not permanently this bar may be covered by the tide.

tranchet A chisel-ended artefact with a sharp, straight working edge, produced by the removal of a flake at right angles to the main axis of the tool.

transepts The transverse parts of a cruciform or cross-shaped church, considered apart from the nave e.g. north transept and south transept.

whin sill A hard, igneous rock formation which outcrops at various places in the northeast of England, especially on the Northumbrian coast and the North Pennines.

Index

INDEX